THE NEW MOTORCYCLE YEARBOOK

2

THE NEW MOTORCYCLE YEARBOOK

2

The Definitive Annual Guide to All New Motorcycles Worldwide Simon de Burton

MERRELL

LONDON · NEW YORK

MERRELL

First published 2006 by
Merrell Publishers Limited

Head office
81 Southwark Street
London SE1 0HX
Email mail@merrellpublishers.com

New York office
49 West 24th Street, 8th Floor
New York, NY 10010
Email info@merrellpublishersusa.com

merrellpublishers.com

Publisher Hugh Merrell
Editorial Director Julian Honer
US Director Joan Brookbank
Sales and Marketing Manager Kim Cope
Associate Manager, US Sales and Marketing
   Elizabeth Choi
Art Director Nicola Bailey
Designer Paul Shinn
Managing Editor Anthea Snow
Project Editors Claire Chandler,
   Rosanna Fairhead
Editor Helen Miles
Production Manager Michelle Draycott
Production Controller Sadie Butler

ISBN-13: 978-1-8589-4339-8
ISBN-10: 1-8589-4339-6

Produced by Merrell Publishers Limited
Designed by Untitled
Copyedited by Richard Dawes

Printed and bound in Singapore

Page 2
Buell Lightning XB12S Long, see pp. 148–49
Pages 4–5
ENV (Emissions Neutral Vehicle), see
pp. 228–29
Pages 8–9
Yamaha YZF-R1SP, see pp. 64–65
Pages 20–21
Yamaha FJR1300 AS, see pp. 30–31
Pages 32–33
Yamaha YZF-R1, see pp. 64–65
Pages 68–69
BMW HP-2, see pp. 72–73
Pages 94–95
Harley-Davidson FLSTI Heritage Softail,
see pp. 98–99
Pages 120–21
Buell Ulysses, see pp.124–25
Pages 132–33
Kawasaki ZZ-R1400, see pp. 138–39
Pages 140–41
Buell Lightning XB12S Long, see pp. 148–49
Pages 188–89
Ducati Sport 1000, see pp. 190–91
Pages 200–201
Yamaha X-Max, see pp. 218–19
Pages 220–21
ENV (Emissions Neutral Vehicle), see
pp. 228–29
Pages 268–69
Yamaha YZF-R6, see pp. 66–67
Page 270
Aprilia RSV-R Mille, see pp. 36–37

CONTENTS

TRENDS, HIGHLIGHTS, AND PREDICTIONS

When we were drawing up the list of entries for *The New Motorcycle Yearbook 2* it soon became apparent that the world's manufacturers are working faster than ever to create interesting new designs, more efficient engines, and generally more refined machines. There are far more new models being made than ever before, so for practical purposes we have restricted the number discussed to 100. Had we been able to include every new motorcycle of every size and type introduced anywhere in the world during the past year, this book could have weighed as much as a fully loaded Honda Gold Wing.

So we have omitted many models, notably the lightweight commuter bikes and scooters made by the myriad manufacturers in China and India. Most of these machines are not, strictly speaking, new, but rebadged clones of such Japanese stalwarts as Honda's CG125 and Vespa's PX, made under license by the Chinese in particular. Yet, while these copies currently have something of a reputation for being put together with less attention to detail than that afforded to the machines from which they were derived, it seems inevitable that China is set to become a major force in the world of "serious" motorcycle manufacture.

Already the giant Qianjiang group, China's largest motorcycle company, has taken control of Benelli, and with such firms as Hongdou making crated 125-cc trail bikes available in Europe via the Internet for around $1300— less than a third of the price of its Japanese rivals—the established brands are looking nervously over their shoulders.

At the 2005 Milan motorcycle show a large proportion of the exhibiting manufacturers were from China, and many are looking to a future of building large-capacity sports bikes, trail bikes, and all-round vehicles. This is a nation famous for the ability of its people to reproduce virtually anything made elsewhere, on a giant scale and at a fraction of the cost: for example, a Chinese carmaker recently launched its own version of the $460,000 Rolls-Royce Phantom that is due to go on the market for half the price. It is very likely that Chinese replicas of such machines as Yamaha's R1 and Honda's CBR600 and Gold Wing are not far behind.

For the time being, however, Japanese and European manufacturers continue to dominate the motorcycle scene and, just as it has been for decades, the market is led by the "big four" Japanese brands and Germany's BMW. Nevertheless, as motorcycling becomes as much a lifestyle statement as a way of getting from A to B, the smaller manufacturers are gradually winning customers over.

Triumph, for example, has been a great success story. One of its most popular machines is the almost cartoonlike Rocket III cruiser (pp. 114–15), which has become a top seller in America, while the Bonneville has attracted born-again riders worldwide. Tue Mantoni, the firm's commercial director, attributes much of the positive reaction to the rekindled brand to the fact that it offers something different from the mainstream opposition. "Our bikes are quite distinct from other makes," he says. "They are defined by having

It seems inevitable that China is set to become a major force in the world of "serious" motorcycle manufacture.

Above
Honda's DN-01 will feature a revolutionary hydraulic gearbox.

parallel twin and three-cylinder engines instead of the v-twin or four-cylinder engines of our competitors and, because Triumph is the oldest motorcycle brand around, the products offer a character and solidity that the volume producers simply do not have.

"We have tried to make the most of Triumph's past by reintroducing such models as the Bonneville and its variants the Thruxton and the Scrambler because the retro trend is very strong at the moment—but you don't get a cool and sexy motorcycle by simply copying what was made during the 1960s. You have to create a fresh and modern interpretation of the past.

"The Rocket III has been very significant in the growth of the brand by drawing totally new customers to our shops and, because it is so unusual-looking and has such a huge engine, it has given us a voice in the media which has really opened people's eyes to Triumph. This has created what you could call a 'halo' effect across the range and brought us a much younger audience."

This strong product range—which offers models from the class-leading Sprint ST touring bike to the retro-styled Bonneville and the mean-looking Speed Triple street machine—is also backed up by Triumph's new "Go Your Own Way" marketing strategy, aimed at capitalizing on the brand's individuality. A swanky revamped image for its dealerships, under the "Triumph World" name, gets away from the traditional bike-shop image of gas fumes and grime, and includes not just Triumph motorcycles but an entire range of lifestyle clothing and accessories to go with them.

Yet, while great-looking but essentially traditional motorcycles are still well received by the buying public, manufacturers know that the bikers of the not-too-distant future will be riding very different machines. Look in the Oddballs section of this book and you will find electric motorcycles, a hydrogen-fuel-cell machine, and one that runs on LPG (pp. 220–39). This is merely the tip of the iceberg: Yamaha, for example, aims to have a hybrid gas/electric bike on sale by 2010 using similar technology to that employed so successfully by Toyota in its Prius and Lexus RX300H cars.

Already Yamaha has produced a concept machine called the Gen-Ryu. This has a powerful 600-cc engine from the R6 sports bike that takes over from a silent, ultra-efficient electric motor once a certain speed is exceeded. By the time the Gen-Ryu reaches the production stage it is likely that it will feature a battery recharging system that operates on kinetic energy from the brakes, a vehicle-to-vehicle warning system and a rearview camera.

A development that is far closer to production is two-wheel drive for motorcycles. Initially aimed at improving traction for off-road machines, this innovation could soon find its way on to road bikes. The American firm Christini has invented a fully mechanical system that takes drive from the motorcycle's gearbox to turn a shaft running inside the frame and up to the headstock. Here a concealed geartrain rotates two further shafts that pass down the outside of the fork legs to power the front hub. Initially Christini's system is likely to be made available as a bolt-on addition for certain production machines, although Yamaha has also been developing a hydraulic two-wheel-drive system that should be in production on its off-road range within three years.

The Japanese firm is also leading the way in "fly-by-wire" electronic throttle technology, the first production examples of which can be seen on the new R6 featured in the Sports Bikes section (pp. 66–67), and it has been one of the first to introduce, with its FJR1300 tourer, a semi-automatic, push-button gearshift system on a road bike (pp. 30–31). Expect to see the system on sports bikes before too long—and don't be surprised if it is adopted across the board: nowadays even relatively modest cars have push-button gearshifting, a feature once seen only on Formula One racers.

But why shift gears at all? Maxi scooters have proved that fully automatic gearboxes work well on engines of 500 cc or more, so why not use them on "full-size" motorcycles? Honda, for one, is well on the way to perfecting an electronically operated clutch and gearshift system that uses hydraulic drive for smoothness and reliability, and it has already installed the technology in its DN-01 concept machine. The peculiarly named HFT (Human Fitting Transmission) system relies on a hydraulic pump that forces fluid into a drive unit at the front of the driveshaft. The fluid flow is electronically altered to govern the speed of the bike independently of engine revs, and the drive unit has three switchable modes: "twist and go" for town

use, six-speed automatic for open roads, and a manual override with handlebar-mounted shifter for sports riding.

In some cases, however, the future of motorcycle engineering appears to lie in looking backward. It has been rumored that Honda is planning to return to a method of power-boosting that was last seen on bikes (and quickly abandoned) in the 1980s. The firm has shown a large-capacity, v-twin concept cruiser that appears to be fitted with a turbocharger.

Turbochargers, which recycle exhaust gas to force-feed fuel into the engine at high revs, were first used by Honda on its CX500 touring bike of 1982 to provide additional overtaking power in the mid-range. The technology was also used by Yamaha on its XJ650 Turbo, Suzuki on its XN85, and Kawasaki on its Z1000. None of the applications was particularly successful, although Kawasaki came close to perfecting it with the short-lived GPz750 turbo sports bike of 1985.

Back then, the lack of success stories about two-wheeled turbos was more attributable to the inability of the engines they were attached to than to the unreliability of the turbos themselves. Now, however, with tougher, freer-spinning engines capable of staying in one piece under much higher loads, the new generation of lightweight turbochargers offers potentially thrilling performance gains.

But with enhanced performance must come greater attention to safety, as instanced by Honda's introduction of the groundbreaking airbag system,

which features on the Gold Wing in the Tourers section (pp. 26–27). It was a brave and bold move by the manufacturer to come out with the airbag, as others, notably BMW and Yamaha, have shied away from it, fearing the obvious consequences of a bag deploying when not needed.

BMW, however, has embarked on a project with KTM to develop a type of carbon-fiber "neck damper" that locates beneath the bottom of a rider's crash helmet to absorb the impact in a serious fall, reducing the degree of sudden movement and therefore the likelihood of injury to neck, head or spine.

But, even if you're riding a motorcycle equipped with an airbag and wearing the best safety gear, there is a high chance of serious injury if one of your tires blows out at high speed—and that is why Michelin has created its new airless motorcycle wheel and tire combination. Maintenance-free, everlasting, and far safer than a conventional air-filled tire, the Michelin Airless Wheel is made from composite radial bands that are part of the wheel. To these is attached a replaceable tread that is cheaper than a conventional tire and still useable even if it becomes cut or damaged.

Even more radical—but far less likely actually to appear on a production machine—is a motorcycle that does not have tires at all but "caterpillar" tracks. The poisonously named Hyanide, designed by Germans Tilmann Schlootz and Oliver Keller, is intended for use in extreme conditions, such as in deserts and at the poles. A single, wide track gives the Hyanide the

maneuverability of a two-wheeler with the traction of a snowmobile.

It sounds like one machine that shouldn't be affected by the latest safety device being planned for both cars and motorcycles: a spy-in-the-sky speed detector that could find its way on to all new production vehicles before the end of the next decade. An electronic map fitted to the vehicle communicates with satellites and can take over to slow the machine down if speed limits are exceeded.

Yet, with the face of Big Brother looming ever larger, it is refreshing to see that some bike builders are disregarding caution and continuing to create the type of wild and crazy machines on which motorcycling has built a reputation for individualism during more than a century. As this book goes to print, German designer Clemens Leonhardt is probably struggling to fit yet another giant component to the prototype of his radical Leonhardt Gunbus, a veritable monster of a motorcycle powered by a 6.7-liter aero engine that is expected to produce around 260 kW (349 bhp).

The frame tubes will be as thick as scaffolding poles and the front and rear wheels will be 34 in. (86 cm) and 37 in. (94 cm) in diameter respectively, and fitted with aircraft tires. The completed machine is expected to dwarf the Triumph Rocket III, currently the world's largest-engined production motorcycle.

Equipped with machines like the Gunbus, we motorcyclists could take over the world and at last our future would be assured.

Above left and center, top and bottom
The Gunbus takes shape.
Above
Michelin's Airless Wheel promises tires for life.

MOTORCYCLING: GRAB IT WHILE YOU CAN

Looking at the machines in this latest edition of *The New Motorcycle Yearbook*, it is obvious that standards of design and engineering are set to continue improving into the foreseeable future. Motorcycles get faster, lighter, more reliable, and more interesting all the time, and the pace of development has been particularly rapid of late.

Yet, to me at least, one fact stands out as remarkable: motorcycles have remained essentially unchanged for a century. True, we now take such features as fuel injection, antilock braking systems, super-powerful engines and aerodynamic fairing for granted, but for all that we're still riding around on a saddle, steering with handlebars, and driving the rear wheel with an internal combustion engine, just as tweed-suited Edwardian motorcyclists did in the early 1900s.

And for that I give thanks, for if motorcycles still exist in a recognizable form at the dawn on the 22nd century, they are far more likely to be powered by a method such as that used in the ENV bike or the electric Vectrix, both featured in the Oddballs section of this book (pp. 220–39). In other words, riders of the future won't be using soulful motorcycles but silent, pollution-free "transport units" designed to be purely functional and not the least bit emotional.

This means that we should be positively reveling in the amazing array of bikes that manufacturers are offering us today, buying them, riding them, and enjoying them. We should be growing the population of motorcyclists and spreading the word that powered two-wheelers not only are practical and fun but, even with internal combustion engines, might just help prolong the future of life as we know it. A life, that is, in which you can walk out your front door and ride somewhere without suffering from, and contributing to, pointless traffic jams and needless pollution.

Anyone who lives in a major city will have observed the explosion in the number of people riding to work on scooters and lightweight motorcycles. Indeed, this trend is helping to speed the wheels of commerce in such fast-developing countries as India and China and, through the Riders for Health organization, bikes are making a vital contribution to the distribution of medical supplies in rural African communities.

In the UK the motorcycling population has risen by around a third in the past decade and, although sales during the past couple of years have slowed considerably since the halcyon days of the late 1990s, the Motorcycle Industry Association's figures for 2004–05 show an overall rise of 6%.

Many of these people—the majority, in fact—take to two wheels more for convenience than out of a long-held desire to start motorcycling, but very often they find it turns into an irresistible passion. They start with a scooter, trade up to a lightweight commuter bike, and end up on a full-size sports machine or, more likely, a sports tourer (sales in this category have risen 10% in a year in the UK) or an adventure sports model (UK annual sales grew by 32% in 2005).

Once they have "done" motorcycling, many people

Riders of the future won't be using soulful motorcycles but silent, pollution-free 'transport units' designed to be purely functional and not in the least bit emotional.

Above
Handlebars, two wheels and an engine: motorcycles of the early 1900s have plenty in common with machines of the twenty-first century.

Above
The fuel of the future? ENVs use a hydrogen fuel cell to provide power for an electric motor for silent, emission-free running.

find it hard to understand how they ever managed without it. The fact is, motorcycling is addictive, it is fun, it is practical, it is economical. Yes, it can be dangerous, but a properly trained and competent rider with his or her wits about them should be able to anticipate and avoid most accidents.

And, of course, motorcycles with internal combustion engines do emit CO_2 but, thanks to super-efficient fuel mapping, ultra-lean-burn engines, and catalytic converters (now found on even the tiniest engines), the quantities are minuscule, even compared with an average-size family hatchback, let alone a high-performance sports car or SUV.

But, despite all these positive aspects and clear benefits, there are bureaucrats who are hell-bent on stopping a perfectly civilized section of society from going about its eminently sensible business. A typical example of this can be seen in London, where mayor Ken Livingstone's Congestion Charge "think tank" has mooted the idea of making users of motorcycles and scooters pay for the privilege of entering the city's central zone.

If you agree that a motorcycle, which takes up a small amount of road space, puts out minimal emissions, and can potentially transport two people—double the number usually seen in commuter cars—is potentially a way to reduce congestion, then surely you would be doing all you could to encourage its use. The spurious reason for the proposal to charge motorcyclists, however, is that the increasing use of powered

two-wheelers in London has led to a marked rise in the number of road-traffic injuries and this needs to be paid for. As someone who rides a motorcycle in the capital at least five days a week, I can't say I have noticed a proliferation of accidents involving motorcycles, but maybe there's a part of London I do not visit that is a sort of two-wheeled, accident-infested version of the Bermuda Triangle.

Yet the sad truth is that we in Britain actually enjoy relative freedom to ride our motorcycles—for now at least. In the summer of 2005, European Union officials proposed a range of restrictive new license laws that, among other things, would raise the minimum age for "direct access" tests (after passing which a newly qualified rider may ride a machine of unlimited engine capacity) from twenty-one to twenty-four and limit riders below the age of nineteen to 125-cc machines. In the event, the proposals, which were part of the Third European Driving License Directive, were put on hold, along with voting on the subject.

But things are already looking bad for motorcyclists in The Netherlands, Germany, and Austria. Around 200 roads in the last of these countries have been closed to bikes on the grounds that they are too dangerous and that they are in areas where the noise of motorcycles is not acceptable!

And then, of course, there is the Vision Zero theory, being supported in Sweden, which aims to reduce vehicle fatalities to nil. This goal, according to its originator, Claes Tingvall, can be achieved only by

banning motorcycles altogether. And British safety experts have suggested that it should be made illegal to ride a motorcycle wearing anything other than European Community-approved safety clothing.

History tells us that this last suggestion is unlikely to be readily accepted, however. Way back in 1988, when the UK government wanted to make leg protectors a compulsory feature of all new motorcycles, the British Motorcyclists Federation (BMF) and the Motorcycle Action Group (MAG) produced a 100,000-signature petition against the idea and 25,000 people attended a rally for riders' rights in London's Hyde Park.

Yet what may be in the cards over the coming years is a tightening up of the way motorcycles look, again for alleged safety reasons. We all know how similar modern cars have become, and this is largely to do with strict crash-test criteria dictating that everything must be smooth and curvy. But, as a flick through the illustrations in this book will immediately show you, motorcycles have so far been allowed to retain their individuality.

Admittedly, race replicas often look very similar, mainly for aerodynamic and ergonomic reasons, but most enthusiasts can usually tell one from another, even if the make emblems are concealed. But, in the many other categories, there are machines of all shapes, sizes, and engine configurations. Look, for example, at BMW's R1200 GS and then compare it with, say, Buell's Ulysses. They are from the same category and have similar specifications, but one could never be confused with the other.

If what you have just read sounds gloomy, please don't despair: the end of the road for motorcycling as we know it is, let's hope, a very long way off. Besides, the really good news is that the old image of motorcyclists as oily-fingernailed, antisocial dropouts appears, finally, to have been laid to rest. For motorcycling has now evolved from being something that people simply did, into a "lifestyle" option. The inherent coolness of bikes is being exploited to great effect by marketing men who have taken the concept of biking chic and extended it to branded clothing and accessories. In some cases they have even ensured a global brand image for a make by designing stores that are instantly recognizable the moment you walk into one, wherever in the world it may be.

This is something Harley-Davidson has been doing for years (you can buy anything from Harley-Davidson-branded dog bowls to pool tables), but now such firms as Triumph have taken the theory on board and, by combining it with some well-placed lifestyle PR and, of course, a wide and covetable range of bikes, the British firm has seen sales rocket way beyond expectations.

In Italy, for example, modern-day Triumph has become something of a biking cult. At the 2005 Triumph weekend held at the Varano race circuit in northern Italy, it appeared to me as if the brand had taken over the number-one spot from Ducati in the hearts of Italy's bikers, although surely that was just an illusion.

But it is not just a matter of selling motorcycles: it is as much about selling the idea of what a motorcycle can

do for you, and nowhere is there better evidence of this than in the knock-on effect of actor Ewan McGregor and his biking pal Charley Boorman's Long Way Round tour aboard BMW GS Adventures. Before the pair set off in April 2004 to ride from London to New York via Russia and Alaska, there was only mediocre interest in their plan, which was hatched both for the pure thrill of the adventure and also to raise funds for the children's charity UNICEF.

By the time the two had finished their odyssey almost four months and 22,000 miles later, worldwide interest had grown, and once Sky television had released a six-hour documentary film of the trip, it became a talking point among bikers and non-bikers alike around the world. The Long Way Round has since been aired no fewer than thirty times; DVD versions of the programs have sold more than 400,000 copies around the world; and a journal recounting the adventure has sold more than 700,000 copies. The 32% rise in the UK sales of adventure sports bikes mentioned earlier has been largely attributed to McGregor and Boorman sparking interest in overlanding.

So the good news is that people are buying bikes and really using them. Those who aren't overlanding are taking their sports bikes to some of the many track days and track-day vacations being organized throughout the world; others are using off-road and trail motorcycles to explore the green lanes of the countryside (usually responsibly, despite what the anti-trail-riding lobby might say); and riders with racing in their blood but

not much cash are taking advantage of the increasing number of supermoto events being scheduled.

Then there is motocross, trials riding—perhaps the most skilled, and most affordable, of motorcycle sports—classic racing, grasstrack, speedway, and a recent growth of interest in flat-track racing. Also on the increase are organized group motorcycling vacations, which often reintroduce biking to former riders who gave up making use of their licenses years ago.

So what are you waiting for? The motorcycles are in here and there is a whole world out there in which to use them, so let's combine the two and take advantage of one of the last great expressions of freedom while we can.

Above (all)
Charley Boorman and Ewan McGregor boosted the popularity of adventure motorcycling with their epic 'Long Way Round' tour.

THE MOTORCYCLES

TOURERS

Readers of the UK edition of the first *New Motorcycle Yearbook* may recall the cover picture showing the BMW K1200 S, the firm's highly acclaimed road-burning supersports machine. It seemed inevitable that such a highly developed and capable engine would soon find its way into other models in the range, and the first to receive it is the all-new K1200 GT tourer. This now gives BMW a lineup of three four-cylinder, 1200-cc globe-shrinkers, the third being the vast and supercomfortable K1200 LT.

Despite its "touring" tag, the K1200 GT is by far the most powerful bike in its class, with its output of 125 kW (167 bhp). However, the engine is essentially the same as that of its more sporting brother; it has simply been detuned slightly to make it better suited to daylong, stress-free cruising at three-figure speeds. And while the machine is undeniably large—a feature that contributes to its extreme comfort and high-speed stability but makes it a bit of a handful around town—it handles beautifully once under way, thanks to the use of the same frame and Paralever (rear) and Duolever (front) suspension systems as are used on the sportier S model.

Further evidence that the K1200 GT is dedicated to enabling its rider and passenger to cover huge distances in the utmost comfort can be seen in the standard furnishing of adjustable seat and handlebars and an electronically controlled windshield, all of which combine to allow an owner to tailor the machine to suit his or her build and preferred riding position.

Every K1200 GT is supplied with touring luggage as standard, while BMW's sophisticated Electronic Suspension Adjustment (ESA), which permits damper alterations to be made from the handlebars, is available as an optional extra.

BMW K1200 GT

Engine
1157 cc, liquid-cooled, double-overhead-camshaft, four-cylinder, sixteen-valve, four-stroke
Power
113 kW (152 bhp) @ 9500 rpm
Torque
130 Nm (100 ft lb) @ 7750 rpm
Gearbox
Six-speed
Final drive
Shaft
Weight
547 lb (249 kg)
Top speed
152 mph (240 km/h)

HONDA DEAUVILLE NTV700

Engine
680 cc, liquid-cooled, single-overhead-camshaft, 52-degree v-twin, four-stroke
Power
38 kW (51 bhp) @ 8000 rpm
Torque
66 Nm (49 ft lb) @ 6500 rpm
Gearbox
Five-speed
Final drive
Chain
Weight
520 lb (236 kg) (527 lb/239 kg with ABS)
Top speed
118 mph (190 km/h)

Honda's Deauville has been something of an unsung hero of the range since it first appeared in 1998. Based on the utilitarian but famously reliable and long-lived NTV600 shaft-drive all-round vehicle, the Deauville was created as a practical, middleweight tourer that was also both slim and light enough for in-town commuting. Glamorous it never was, and it was never meant to be.

One of the Deauville's radical features—if such an adjective can rightly be used of this most low-key of motorcycles—was its ingenious integrated pannier system, which blended seamlessly with the machine and gave it its distinctive, if unremarkable, appearance.

This latest version not only is considerably more eye-catching, but is faster, more powerful, and even more practical. The engine capacity has been boosted by 33 cc and overall weight has been reduced by the use of a new, twin-spar frame mounted with a broader, more wind-cheating fairing and a two-position screen.

Redesigned instruments with a large, midmounted LCD display make for an up-to-the minute dashboard arrangement, while those trademark built-in panniers can now hold an extra 10 liters (0.35 cu. ft), while retaining their handy connecting "through hole" for the storage of smaller items. There's extra space in the fairing, too, courtesy of one-touch glove boxes that nestle behind the piggyback, multireflector headlights.

It may not have the cult following of the Gold Wing or the ability to cruise effortlessly all day long at 130 mph (209 km/h), like some of the bigger supertourers, but for practical, real-world motorcycling the Deauville has always been hard to beat, and this new version seems likely to set the bar several notches higher.

Its lazy, v-twin engine offers a more than adequate cruising speed combined with excellent fuel economy and, if it is anything like its predecessor, the Deauville NTV700 is virtually guaranteed to get you where you want to go with the minimum of fuss and with total long-term reliability. Indeed it is not unusual to see older versions of Honda's brilliant v-twin still going strong after more than 250,000 miles (400,000 km).

With its throne-like seating, integrated entertainment system, weather-beating fairing, and whisper-quiet 1800-cc engine, it's hard to believe that the Honda Gold Wing, the king of touring bikes, could be made any more luxurious. Yet the already mind-boggling specification has now been enhanced by the addition of the first airbag system ever to be offered on a production motorcycle.

Since the Gold Wing has long been famed for having more gadgets than any other bike, it seems only right that this safety aid from the car world should make its two-wheeled debut on Honda's flagship.

In the event of a head-on crash, a quartet of sensors mounted on the front fork measure the change in speed caused by the impact and, in a split second, convey the data to a dedicated airbag ECU (electronic control unit) that decides, equally quickly, whether or not to deploy the airbag. If the answer is "affirmative," the entire operation takes place in just 0.06 seconds.

Honda has spent thousands of hours testing the airbag at its state-of-the-art Real World Crash Test Facility, using computerized simulation and the first realistic motorcycle crash test dummies, so the chances of an accidental deployment should be zero.

Other improvements to the machine include the fitting of Honda's Linear Air Fuel (LAF) low emission system, which, despite the fact that the Gold Wing's engine is considerably larger than that of many cars, ensures that the bike produces less than half of the amount of harmful emissions allowed by stringent new Euro Three limits.

A throttle-actuated cruise control has also been added, along with a "Comfort Package" that really does complete the Gold Wing's image as a "two-wheeled limousine": it features electric heating for the seats and pillion backrest, which can be warmed to any one of six temperatures up to a maximum of 104° F (40° C). The system also heats the handlebar grips and provides a flow of warm air over the rider's feet. The outlaw bikers of olden days would surely have sneered at the thought.

HONDA GOLD WING 1800

Engine
1832 cc, liquid-cooled, six-cylinder, twelve-valve, four-stroke
Power
87 kW (116 bhp) @ 5500 rpm
Torque
167 Nm (123 ft lb) @ 4000 rpm
Gearbox
Five-speed overdrive with electric reverse
Final drive
Shaft
Weight
886 lb (402 kg)
Top speed
140 mph (225 km/h)

MOTO GUZZI NORGE 1200

Engine
1133 cc, air-cooled, v-twin, four-stroke
Power
66 kW (89 bhp) @ 7500 rpm
Torque
95 Nm (70 ft lb) @ 6800 rpm
Gearbox
Six-speed
Final drive
Shaft
Weight
542 lb (246 kg)
Top speed
125 mph (201 km/h)

Moto Guzzi has always had a loyal following among those who like so-called "real" motorcycles. The Italian firm's insistence on continuing to fit its bikes with what are essentially outdated 90-degree v-twin, air-cooled engines has lent the make a charm and identity that would surely be lost if any other configuration were used.

With the Norge, however, Moto Guzzi is hoping to go head to head with the likes of BMW and Honda's high-tech touring bikes , a move that required the upgrading of the venerable v-twin, which, although it looks very similar to Guzzi engines of yesteryear, has been totally reworked from the ground up.

Much like Harley-Davidson fans, Guzzi riders love the raw feel and sound of the air-cooled engine and this was an important factor in the development of the Norge: it needed to be sophisticated enough to be a practical and effective tourer, but it had to be pure Moto Guzzi, too. To this end, the capacity was increased to 1133 cc, which provides a relatively modest peak horsepower—far less than the 93 kW (125 bhp) of BMW's rival R1200 ST—but enough low-down torque to make it a relaxed road-eater.

The model's significance in the new Guzzi lineup is reflected in the fact that it is named after the original touring bike built by Giuseppe Guzzi in the late 1920s, on which he rode from his base at Mandello del Lario up to the Norwegian Arctic Circle.

Old man Guzzi would find the journey much more comfortable on the twenty-first-century Norge, with its large, aerodynamically designed fairing that has an electrically adjustable screen and wind-deflecting leg shields. He would also appreciate the color-matched hard luggage that is fitted to the bike as standard and has been thoughtfully designed to be narrower than the rearview mirrors. Anyone who has ridden through dense traffic on a bike with panniers will know how easy it is to forget that they are there until it's too late.

The Norge also offers GPS navigation and Bluetooth wireless technology, which enables a mobile telephone to be used safely while on the move. Antilock brakes come as standard, although the feature can be deactivated if the rider chooses, and the Norge's generous 23-liter (5 gallons) fuel tank gives it a more than useful range of up to 298 miles (480 km) between gas stops. Truly a supertourer with personality.

Only the eagle-eyed are likely to spot the difference between this latest version of Yamaha's big touring bike and the one that has been named "Bike of the Year" three years running by a top European motorcycle magazine—but take a close look at that left-hand switchgear.

"AS" after the FJR model designation denotes that this version is fitted with Yamaha's revolutionary YCC-S system, short for Yamaha Chip Controlled Shift, an electronic, semiautomatic gearshift.

Semiautomatic gearboxes controlled from steering-wheel-mounted "paddles" originated in Formula One car racing and have been available in the mainstream automotive world for some years now, but this is the first time the idea has been applied to a roadgoing bike.

Yamaha claims the YCC-S offers "journey enhancing technology" by allowing the rider to use a handlebar-mounted shifter to deliver superfast gear changes without the need to disengage the clutch manually. Traditionalists, meanwhile, can still choose to shift gears using the conventionally mounted foot lever, again without having to disengage the clutch.

How the world's hard-riding tourists will take to the system remains to be seen. Pulling in a clutch lever and blipping the throttle before executing a seamless downshift as one cants a bike into a flowing bend is, for many, part of what motorcycling is all about.

The automotive world has certainly embraced the idea of electronic shifters, so it seems likely that they will become more commonplace on motorcycles. But let's not forget that Honda produced far cruder versions of the clutchless motorcycle during the late 1970s in the form of the Dream 400 AT and the CB750 auto. They crashed and burned, partly because most riders couldn't see the point of them and partly because it was feared that they might go wrong and cost a fortune to fix.

But I'm sure that after riding the supersophisticated FJR1300AS for a few hundred miles and growing used to its smooth, fluidlike gearshifts, all but the most hard-bitten Luddites will come to regard the once second-nature action of pulling in a handlebar-mounted clutch lever and flicking a rod with your foot as a rather quaint chore that they can easily live without.

YAMAHA FJR1300AS

Engine
1298 cc, liquid-cooled, double-overhead-camshaft, sixteen-valve, four-stroke
Power
106 kW (142 bhp) @ 8000 rpm
Torque
134 Nm (99 ft lb) @ 7000 rpm
Gearbox
Five-speed with clutchless, electronic shifting system
Final drive
Shaft
Weight
591 lb (268 kg)
Top speed
160 mph (257 km/h)

SPORTS
BIKES

APRILIA RS125

Engine
124 cc, liquid-cooled, single-cylinder, two-stroke
Power
27 kW (36 bhp) @ 11,500 rpm
Torque
20 Nm (15 ft lb) @ 10,000 rpm
Gearbox
Six-speed
Final drive
Chain
Weight
265 lb (120 kg)
Top speed
100 mph (161 km/h)

The sun began to set on the era of the two-stroke sports bike way back in the early 1990s, but one little machine has clung on, to become something of a legend: Aprilia's fun-packed RS125.

Once they become qualified to ride a "full-size" bike, most motorcyclists can't wait to leave the world of small-capacity machines far behind them, but anyone who hasn't spent a sunny afternoon in the company of an RS125 on a stretch of mountain switchbacks has not enjoyed one of biking's finer moments.

The RS125 offers sublime handling, eye-popping brakes, and a superb power-to-weight ratio. What more could anyone ask for in a sports-oriented motorcycle? How about fabulous looks? Well, the RS has got those, too, thanks to a total makeover that gives the latest version all the appearance of its much bigger brother, the RSV-R Mille, in miniature.

Everything from the fuel tank to the seat and fairing has been developed in a wind tunnel on the basis that, with a lightweight, small-engined machine such as this, every bit of drag that can be eliminated should result in a marked boost in performance.

And, like many bigger bikes, the RS125 also has an onboard computer that can be activated from handlebar-mounted switches to give readings for speed and engine coolant temperature as well as lap-time statistics. There is even a transponder-style optical sensor that provides extremely accurate lap rate recording during real racing.

But you won't need to take to the track to enjoy the RS125 to the full. Its screaming 27-kW (36 bhp), single-cylinder engine just begs to be revved and the race-style brakes and forks allow the bike to be leaned over at angles far steeper than most riders would ever dare to explore.

For those who want to take it to the limit, however, Aprilia also offers a track-only tuning kit, comprising a race exhaust, alternative power valve, larger carburetor, and a harder sparkplug. A special Italian race series for teenagers has been designed around the machine.

At one time the default choice of lovers of large-capacity Italian sports bikes was Ducati's range-topping 916 and its offspring the 996, 998, and 999. But when Aprilia launched its first RSV Mille in 1998, more than a few former Ducati loyalists jumped ship. Since then, the number of converts has continued to grow, and for many riders the Aprilia's ever-improving standard of finish, its reputation for reliability, and its conservative appearance compared with Ducati's controversially styled 999 are enough to give the Mille the edge.

Two versions have always been available, the standard model and the Factory, the second being an even more sporty variant fitted with higher-quality components. Now the latest Mille has been brought closer to its more exotic brother with the addition of race-quality Ohlins forks, "Y-spoke" wheels, and the same Brembo radial brakes as used on the Factory of 2005.

On both bikes the majority of the bodywork is also new, in particular the lower fairing panels, which have been given much deeper air intakes for improved engine cooling. Buyers of the new Factory get forged wheels that are 25% lighter, weight-saving carbon-fiber mudguards front and rear, carbon fairing panels, and carbon spoilers to flank the headlamps.

Plenty of other small but important details also grace the Factory, such as a nonslip racing seat and an Ohlins track monoshock that is tuned for optimum performance when the bike is ridden solo. But if you're Mille-spotting, the quickest way to tell the two apart will be by the special gold-colored frame finish that is exclusive to the lighter (by 9 lb/4 kg) Factory.

The supertorquey v-twin engine has also been upgraded for both versions, with a boost over the old model of 4 kW (6 bhp), a figure that Aprilia's engineers say improves by a further 2 kW (3 bhp) when the bike is traveling at top speed, thanks to a more efficient ram air intake. But, at over 155 mph (250 km/h), who's going to spot the difference?

APRILIA RSV-R MILLE/RSV-R FACTORY

Engine
997 cc, liquid-cooled, double-overhead-camshaft, 60-degree v-twin, eight-valve, four-stroke
Power
105 kW (141 bhp) @ 10,000 rpm
Torque
101 Nm (74 ft lb) @ 8000 rpm
Gearbox
Six-speed
Final drive
Chain
Weight
Mille 408 lb (185 kg); Factory 399 lb (181 kg)
Top speed
Mille 157 mph (252 km/h); Factory 162 mph (260 km/h)

BENELLI TORNADO 1130 TRE

Engine
1130 cc, liquid-cooled, double-overhead-camshaft, three-cylinder, four-stroke
Power
120 kW (161 bhp) @ 10,500 rpm
Torque
119 Nm (88 ft lb) @ 6800 rpm
Gearbox
Six-speed
Final drive
Chain
Weight
441 lb (200 kg)
Top speed
170 mph (274 km/h) (est.)

High excitement surrounded the arrival of the Benelli Tornado when it was launched in 2000 following the revival of the revered Italian make founded in 1911. However, a high price tag and insufficient investment by its then owners prevented the Tornado from ever becoming a serious contender in the superbike arena. Despite its sublime looks and neat features—in particular its underseat cooling fans—first-generation versions of the Tornado ended up offered at discounts of up to 50% off list price.

Then, in 2005, Benelli was bought by China's largest motorcycle producer, the Qianjiang group. The new owner promised to maintain production at the headquarters in Pesaro while providing the means for the firm to announce the introduction of a seriously upgraded Tornado powered by an engine 230 cc larger than the original.

Whereas the old 900 pushed out an impressive but unremarkable 110 kW (147 bhp), the new 1130 version offers a claimed 120 kW (161 bhp): enough to make it more than a match for its Italian rivals from Ducati and Aprilia and a troublesome new competitor for the Japanese.

The Tornado's direct opposition, however, is the Triumph Daytona 1050, the only other three-cylinder sports bike on the market. The new Tornado engine is based on that of the TNT naked, but has been retuned to give sports-bike edge by adding more than 15 kW (20 bhp) and increasing the rev limit.

Its bodywork and frame might have gone basically unchanged save for some eye-catching new paint schemes, but the Tornado remains one of the most gorgeous-looking sports bikes on the market. And now, thanks to Qianjiang's backing, we might see it made in sufficient numbers to put the Benelli name well and truly back on the world map.

BMW's brutally powerful K1200 S of late 2004 was considered by many to be the first true supersports motorcycle ever produced by the German manufacturer, best known for its high-quality touring machines.

But, as fast and capable as the K1200 S is, it could not really be placed in the same league as established race replicas such as Yamaha's R1 or Honda's Fireblade. The new R1200 S, however, really deserves the sports-bike tag and is a welcome breath of fresh air in a market currently top-heavy with Japanese across-the-frame four-cylinder machines.

The R1200 S uses BMW's legendary air-cooled "boxer" twin configuration, which might seem old-fashioned next to the humming, water-cooled, multi-cylinder competition, yet it has been tuned to rev to 8800 rpm, churn out 91 kW (122 bhp), and produce a stump-pulling 112 Nm (83 ft lb) of torque.

In "real world" riding this means the BMW offers superb pickup from low revs, excellent roll-on acceleration, and a slingshot exit from corners. The sight of those cylinders poking out at either side should not be allowed to give the impression that this bike can't be laid down hard, either: an all-new, superstiff chassis in which the engine is an integrated, load-bearing component makes for pin-sharp handling and quick turning.

The exhaust system tucks in tight beneath the engine, exiting, in current sports-bike style, with a neat, underseat silencer that helps to contribute to the machine's slim profile. Weight has been saved through the use of items such as magnesium fairing supports and an aluminum rear subframe.

The R1200 S also incorporates the latest "CAN-bus" single-wire electronic technology, which drives the bike's Info Flatscreen. Complementing the analog speedo and rev counter, this device allows the rider to call up digital displays relating to everything from fuel range to oil temperature and is automatically adjusted for optimum visibility in varying light conditions by a photocell control unit.

The old R1100 S replaced by this machine proved its worth in a dedicated race series called the Boxer Cup, and, to show that it also intends the 1200 to be ridden in a competitive spirit, BMW is offering optional extras such as Ohlins sports suspension, an extra-wide 6-in. (15 cm) rear wheel fitted with a 7.5-in. (190 mm) section rear tire for added grip, and a sporty hump to cover the pillion seat.

BMW R1200 S

Engine
1170 cc, air-cooled, twin-cylinder, eight-valve, four-stroke
Power
91 kW (122 bhp) @ 8250 rpm
Torque
112 Nm (83 ft lb) @ 6800 rpm
Gearbox
Six-speed
Final drive
Shaft
Weight
419 lb (190 kg)
Top speed
150 mph (241 km/h) (est.)

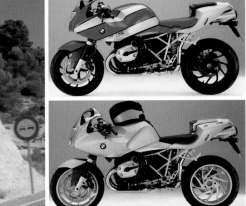

DUCATI DESMOSEDICI

Engine
989 cc, double-overhead-camshaft, four-cylinder, 16-valve, four-stroke
Power
149 kW (200 bhp) plus @ 13,500 rpm
Torque
Not available
Gearbox
Six-speed, cassette type
Final drive
Chain
Weight
Not available
Top speed
200 mph (322 km/h) plus, depending on gearing

Many sports-bike fans dream of being able to ride a genuine Grand Prix racer on the road and a few diehard enthusiasts have converted competition-bred machines for highway use by adding the items needed to make them street legal.

Most of us, however, have to make do with "race replicas" that are much-tamed versions of the genuine GP bikes ridden by heroes of the track. But, with the Desmosedici RR, Ducati is the first manufacturer to offer a true "racer for the road." This 149-kW (200 bhp) fire-breather, with a potential top speed of more than 200 mph (322 km/h), was developed directly from the GP race-bike project embarked on in 2002.

Ducati quit Grand Prix racing during the 1970s but resumed when the rules changed in 2002 to give priority to four-stroke machines. The firm's return led to the development of its first multicylinder engine, the "L" layout, four-cylinder unit that powers the Desmosedici, so called because of its sixteen, Desmodromically operated valves.

Along with the race-bred engine, buyers of the new machine will get a faithful reproduction of the GP6 race bike's carbon-fiber bodywork that dresses the state-of-the-art tubular trellis frame. This, in turn, is mounted on Ohlins GP-quality suspension with Marchesini forged-magnesium wheels fitted with Brembo competition brakes identical to those used on the GP6 for wet-weather racing.

The first Desmosedici RRs are due to hit the streets in July 2007, with an estimated four hundred examples scheduled to be produced each year at a cost of $70,000 each. That might sound like a lot of money for a motorcycle but, when you consider the millions that are poured into the development of GP bikes to make them competitive, the price tag starts to look relatively reasonable. And you do get a race exhaust, bike cover, paddock stand, and decal kit thrown in.

If you're going to own a 999R Xerox, you'll need to be a seriously good rider to live up to the machine's image. This latest version of Ducati's hugely powerful, road-legal racer is as close as you'll get (except for the lights and indicators) to the official factory bikes on which works riders James Toseland and Regis Laconi thunder around some of the world's most famous circuits during the SBK race series.

Machines such as this are built to be appreciated by true race aficionados, who will instantly spot that the 999R Xerox is correct in every detail, down to its black-anodized steering head and footpegs and the small red Brembo racing logos attached to the brake calipers and mounting brackets.

If they are looking at a totally "cloned" machine, race geeks will even spot that the owner has also fitted the additional decals supplied with each bike that allow them to create a red pinline around the racing wheels. Underneath the decoration, however, this new-look 999R is the same as the "ordinary" version—if you can use the word of a bike dressed in carbon-fiber bodywork and powered by an engine that produces 111 kW (149 bhp).

Some "Ducatisti" had been hoping for something entirely fresh for the 2006 model, not just a decal kit, but the firm claims the last batch of alterations took the 999 so much further that this time none was necessary.

The 999R Xerox and its "non-Xeroxed" counterpart are entirely road-legal but, as they are intended for track use, they come with a race kit that includes an earsplitting open-silencer Termignoni exhaust system.

DUCATI 999R XEROX

Engine
999 cc, liquid-cooled, l-twin, eight-valve, four-stroke
Power
111 kW (149 bhp) @ 9750 rpm
Torque
116 Nm (85 ft lb) @ 8000 rpm
Gearbox
Six-speed
Final drive
Chain
Weight
399 lb (181 kg)
Top speed
170 mph (274 km/h)

HONDA CBR1000RR FIREBLADE

Engine
998 cc, liquid-cooled, double-overhead-camshaft, four-cylinder, sixteen-valve, four-stroke
Power
126 kW (169 bhp) @ 11,250 rpm
Torque
115 Nm (85 ft lb) @ 10,000 rpm
Gearbox
Six-speed
Final drive
Chain
Weight
388 lb (176 kg)
Top speed
185 mph (298 km/h) (est.)

When the original Fireblade was launched in 1992, with its winning formula of powerful engine, compact dimensions, and fine handling, it set a standard that enabled the model to remain the sharpest tool in the hyper-performance box for years to come.

Gradually, however, Honda's rivals caught up with and improved upon the 'Blade's specification and lately it is Suzuki's GSX-R1000 that has come to be regarded as the king of the one-liter sports bikes.

Honda obviously doesn't approve of this, so the latest Fireblade is a totally reworked version of the previous model, which itself seemed so radical when it first emerged in 2003 with the long-awaited capacity increase from 900 to almost 1000 cc.

On the new version the engine remains a 998-cc unit, but dotted around the bike there are more than 200 improvements, most of which only the dedicated Fireblade expert would spot at a glance. For a start, small changes to the engine internals—including reshaped and enlarged intake and exhaust ports, a raised compression ratio and the addition of dual valve springs—have boosted the rev limit by 5% to 12,200 rpm.

A stronger, lighter crankshaft helps the motor spin more freely, the radiator has been minimized to reduce mass, the final-drive gear ratio has been lowered to give improved acceleration, and the handling has been sharpened by the use of a steeper steering-head angle.

A new exhaust has also been created, with the sole purpose of making the new Fireblade as lithe as possible—it shaves a vital extra 21 oz (600 g) off the overall weight. Thanks to this and other "slimming aids," such as a new hollow-section cast-aluminum frame, a shorter rear subframe, and lightweight, magnesium engine covers, the bike now tips the scales at a svelte 388 lb (176 kg).

That distinctive Fireblade look, marked by the "fox eye" headlamps, remains largely unchanged, although the fairing has been reworked to provide better airflow to the engine and reduce the amount of heat deflected on to the rider during hard sessions at the track.

The new Fireblade is also the only machine on the road to be equipped with Honda's Electronic Steering Damper (HESD), which sits on top of the steering head and automatically adjusts to changes in surface conditions, speed, and lean angles.

Kawasaki has a long-standing reputation for producing superbikes with class-leading power outputs, but over the years the competition has gradually caught up with and, in some cases, overtaken "the big K." Nevertheless, the power churned out by each of the four main Japanese one-liter supersports bikes is now so prodigious that few riders will ever be able to discover the tiny differences in performance that occur at the upper end of the scale.

But, with the new ZX-10R, Kawasaki has created a machine that puts it back at the top of the power tree, thanks to the awesome 135 kW (181 bhp) that is claimed to be available at the end of the twist grip. What is truly brilliant about this bike, however, is that with all this power it can be as raw and aggressive, or as mild-mannered and gentle, as the rider wishes.

In the lower reaches of the engine's 11,700-rpm range, this machine will trickle through traffic without a hint of complaint. Yet, out on the open road or on the racetrack, it will allow a rider to explore the limits of his or her talent, delivering its full power in a manner that falls just on the comfortable side of frightening.

Harnessing such performance requires an exceptional chassis, and the ZX-10R is built around an all-new, short, lightweight frame, with revised geometry giving greater mass centralization, and fitted with a longer swing arm for extra stability.

This is backed up by a race-quality Ohlins steering damper to control the front-wheel wag that is inevitable under full-bore acceleration, while "petal" brake discs gripped by ultrasharp, radially mounted calipers work in conjunction with a "slipper" clutch to provide instant, safe stopping power from any speed.

The bodywork is all new, too—everything from the ultracompact headlamps to the flush-fitting turn signals and even the somewhat unsightly exhaust system has been wind-tunnel-designed to make the ZX-10R slip through the air as effortlessly as possible.

Kawasaki is calling this "the ultimate Ninja," and so it is—so far.

KAWASAKI ZX-10R NINJA

Engine
998 cc, liquid-cooled, double-overhead-camshaft, four-cylinder, sixteen-valve, four-stroke
Power
135 kW (181 bhp) @ 11,700 rpm
Torque
107 Nm (79 ft lb) @ 9500 rpm
Gearbox
Six-speed
Final drive
Chain
Weight
386 lb (175 kg)
Top speed
185 mph (298 km/h) (est.)

MOTO CZYSZ
C1 990

Engine
989 cc, double-overhead-camshaft, twin-crankshaft, narrow-angle v-four, four-stroke
Power
Not available
Torque
Not available
Gearbox
Six-speed
Final drive
Chain
Weight
401 lb (182 kg) (est.)
Top speed
150 mph (241 km/h) (est.)

Choosing to develop and build your own motorcycle is one thing; aspiring to produce one of the most radical Grand Prix racing machines ever seen is something else. That was the intention of American architect Michael Czysz (pronounced "Sis") when he launched his C1 project in 2003 from a purpose-built facility in Portland, Oregon.

Now in the fine-tuning stage, the C1 is emerging as a far-out racer with a carbon-fiber frame, a radical "flexible" front fork, and an in-line four-cylinder, longitudinally mounted engine with separate, counter-rotating crankshafts. The gearbox is tucked beneath the engine and sends power to the rear wheel through not one but two clutches, while the entire motor measures just 6.5 in. (2.6 cm) in width.

Thanks to advances in computer-aided design and manufacture, Czysz's investment in the project has been, in his words, "incredibly low," at around $2 million. One hundred and fifty street-legal versions of the C1 are scheduled to be available in 2007, priced at around $65,000 each, although the first fifty bikes to be built are destined solely for the racetrack.

Czysz, who has designed houses for Cindy Crawford, Lenny Kravitz, and other celebrities, decided to build his own motorcycle as a "distraction" from his core business. A longtime two-wheeler fanatic who used to race Aprilia RS 250 two-strokes, he has motorcycling in his blood: his grandfather, Clarence, was a successful motorcycle tuner who built Manx Norton race bikes during the 1940s and 1950s.

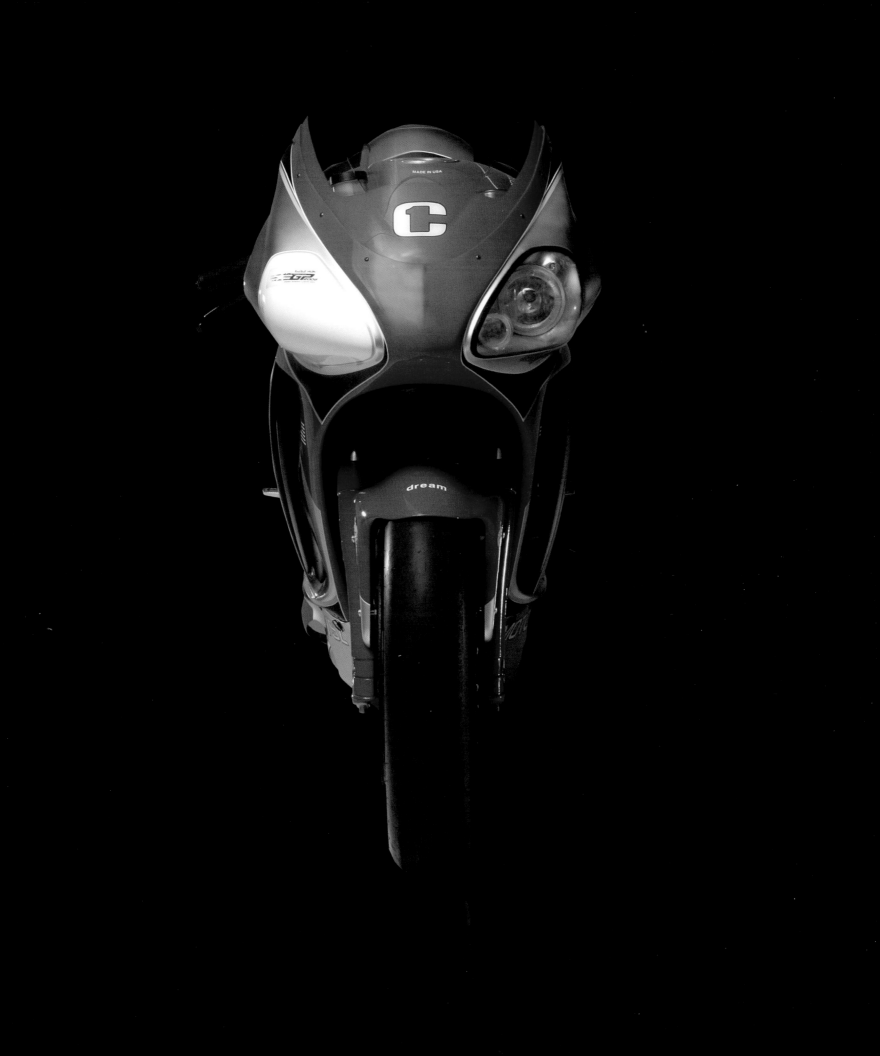

Motor-racing legend Ayrton Senna may be best remembered for his prowess behind a steering wheel, but he was also a keen motorcyclist. As a result, his close friend Claudio Castiglioni—the industrial tycoon formerly behind Ducati and later MV Agusta—has, in the past, instigated the creation of two limited-edition Senna motorcycles: one based on the Ducati 916, the other on the MV Agusta F4 750.

However, this latest tribute machine, based on MV Agusta's ultraexotic F4 1000, can lay claim to being the most powerful motorcycle ever to honor the name of the Formula One hero. A production limit of 300 machines has been set and some of the proceeds will go to the Senna Foundation, a charity for underprivileged children that is run by Senna's sister in the family's native Brazil.

Beneath the special gray, black, and red Senna design that decorates the predominantly carbon-fiber bodywork, this F4 boasts lightweight racing wheels, state-of-the-art Brembo competition brakes, a super-light rear shock absorber, and titanium-nitride-coated forks, all of which help to reduce overall weight by 4 lb (2 kg) as compared with the stock model.

The engine has also been reworked to rev higher than the standard unit and produce 6 kW (8 bhp) more power at 11,900 rpm, although the top speed remains the same, as the final-drive gear ratio has been lowered to take advantage of the extra available revs and to make acceleration even more blistering than that offered by the stock F4 1000.

Readers of the first *New Motorcycle Yearbook* will recall the equally delicious-looking MV Ago and Tamburini limited editions produced by the company. Demand for these far outstripped supply and they have already become collector's items that command a premium. So it seems inevitable that the added cachet provided by the Senna name's presence on the side of this latest model will turn it into a very collectable piece overnight.

The MV Agusta F4 Senna: coming to a museum near you soon.

MV AGUSTA F4 SENNA

Engine
998 cc, liquid-cooled, double-overhead-camshaft, four-cylinder, sixteen-valve, four-stroke
Power
130 kW (174 bhp) @ 11,900 rpm
Torque
111 Nm (82 ft lb) @ 10,000 rpm
Gearbox
Six-speed cassette unit
Final drive
Chain
Weight
419 lb (190 kg)
Top speed
186 mph (300 km/h)

MV AGUSTA VELTRO

Engine
998 cc, liquid-cooled, double-overhead-camshaft, four-cylinder, sixteen-valve, four-stroke
Power
130 kW (174 bhp) @ 12,000 rpm
Torque
117 Nm (86 ft lb) @ 9000 rpm
Gearbox
Six-speed
Final drive
Chain
Weight
375 lb (170 kg)
Top speed
191 mph (307 km/h)

Elsewhere in this section you will find MV Agusta's F4 Senna, the fastest motorcycle ever to bear Senna's name. Here you see the fastest and most powerful road-going motorcycle ever to carry the MV Agusta emblem, the mind-blowingly quick Veltro. And if you ever believed motorcycling wasn't supposed to be elitist, the Veltro might change your opinion: just twenty-three will be built, each carrying a price tag in excess of $55,000.

Based on the Veltro race bike, this road version has a mildly detuned engine to give 130 kW (174 bhp), although with some easily fitted race parts this can quickly be returned to the 138-kW (185 bhp) level of the track version. All bodywork is made from lightweight carbon fiber and the brakes and suspension components are all state-of-the-art racing items.

When the bike was unveiled in Milan in 2005, the show model bore a design in the colors of the Italian Air Force 23rd Fighter Group, members of which were the first to ride the Veltro, which was clocked at 191 mph (307 km/h) on the runway usually reserved for their fighter jets.

MV hopes to enter the World Superbike contest with a 149-kW-plus (200 bhp) racer also based on the F4 engine.

In terms of looks and performance, Aprilia's two-stroke RS 125 has long been the benchmark learner sports bike, but that crown looks likely to be stolen by Rieju's beautifully designed Matrix, one of the best-looking 125-cc race replicas on the market.

In line with modern thinking, the Rieju uses a four-stroke engine to keep emissions to a minimum, but it has been engineered to provide high-revving, two-stroke-style power delivery and, although it is supplied in restricted, 9-kW (12 bhp) form, the unit seems certain to respond well to light tuning.

The frame is derived from the firm's 50-cc, two-stroke sports bike, but since that was overengineered in the first place it does not compromise the 125 in any way. Handling is light and positive and, to enhance the excellent cornering ability of the chassis, only top-quality ancillary parts have been used, such as Michelin Sport Pilot tires, powerful twin-piston brakes front and back, and an adjustable rear shock absorber.

The Matrix is in head-to-head competition with Honda's CBR125R and costs almost the same. No question that it's as good to look at and performs just as well, but it remains to be seen whether or not the brand can compete with the Japanese giant in terms of reliability and aftersales service.

RIEJU MATRIX 125

Engine
123 cc, air-cooled, single-cylinder, four-stroke
Power
9 kW (12 bhp) (restricted)
Torque
Not available
Gearbox
Five-speed
Final drive
Chain
Weight
236 lb (107 kg)
Top speed
70 mph (113 km/h) (est.)

Elsewhere in this section you can read about Yamaha's supercool new R6, the current standard setter in the 600-cc supersports class. Or is it? Suzuki, too, has gone all out to claim the crown with this fabulous, all-new take on the GSX-R600, which the manufacturer claims has been "designed to win championships and road race events across the world."

It certainly has all the right credentials, thanks to an entirely new chassis, a completely revised engine, a race-ready slipper clutch, and an extremely cool cutoff exhaust pipe that exits just below the rider's right foot in the latest race style. The trend for underseat silencers that we have just gotten used to is now, it seems, becoming rather "yesterday."

The thinking behind the creation of this middleweight supersports machine has been to shrink, lighten, and reduce everything as far as is practically possible, to the point where the bike has almost toylike proportions. But there is nothing toylike about its performance, with a 0–60 mph (0–97 km/h) sprint capability of just three seconds and a top speed of 165 mph (265 km/h).

The small size of the bike has, however, prompted Suzuki to provide adjustable rider footpegs to enable it to be tailored to the individual, a particularly important feature now that the shortened wheelbase has greatly reduced the reach from the seat to the handlebars.

On a race-oriented machine such as this, having the space to move about quickly and freely during high-speed directional changes is essential, because feeling at anything less than one with the bike can have a drastic effect on lap times and race performance—and that counts to buyers, even if most will never find themselves lining up on a starting grid with a race to win.

Another feature that has always troubled such wannabe racers is the tiresome presence of directional indicators on their sports bikes. Suzuki, like many other superbike manufacturers, has started integrating the indicators into the bodywork for better aerodynamics and a more discreet look. The front indicators on the GSX-R600 are built into the rearview mirrors.

SUZUKI GSX-R600

Engine
599 cc, liquid-cooled, double-overhead-camshaft, four-cylinder, sixteen-valve, four-stroke
Power
93 kW (125 bhp) @ 13,500 rpm
Torque
68 Nm (50 bhp) @ 11,500 rpm
Gearbox
Six-speed
Final drive
Chain
Weight
355 lb (161 kg)
Top speed
165 mph (265 km/h) (est.)

SUZUKI GSX-R750

Engine
750 cc, liquid-cooled, double-overhead-camshaft, four-cylinder, sixteen-valve, four-stroke
Power
112 kW (150 bhp) @ 13,000 rpm
Torque
52 Nm (67.6 ft lb) @ 12,500 rpm
Gearbox
Six-speed
Final drive
Chain
Weight
359 lb (163 kg)
Top speed
175 mph (282 km/h) (est.)

The first Suzuki GSX-R750 was destined to become an all-time classic when it was launched on an unsuspecting public back in 1985. Emblazoned on the side of its fuel tank was the legend "Hyper Sports," a tag that Suzuki had invented specifically for the bike and that came to represent a new class of machine.

That first GSX-R was, in looks, performance and handling, essentially an endurance racing replica for the road, and it was just what motorcyclists who loved to ride fast had been waiting for after years of putting up with a tedious stream of lumpen, ill-handling, similar-looking Japanese four-cylinder bikes.

The "Gixxer" became a cult machine but, as trends changed, so did engine capacity, and GSX-Rs of 600 cc and 1000 cc overshadowed the 750, while a lack of competition caused by the fact that other manufacturers were largely ignoring the 750-cc class left the Suzuki pretty much in a league of one.

However, this new GSX-R could well revive interest in the 750 arena because it comes within a whisker of the performance of a 1000-cc sports bike, yet has the dimensions, weight, handling, and responsiveness of a 600; in fact, it is actually lighter than some 600s. And what superbike builder would not want to achieve that?

With a lighter, more compact engine that revs higher and makes more power, straighter air intakes for better breathing, race-ready forged pistons, and a shorter, quicker-handling chassis, the new GSX-R is worthy of attaining the legendary status that the original version continues to enjoy.

It looks pretty neat, too, with its trendy triangular-section, stubby exhaust tucked in close to the frame, minimalist three-spoke wheels, and nifty new bodywork that includes a particularly avant-garde flared tail section with built-in turn signals.

Suzuki calls the GSX-R750 its "miniature supersport giant," which sounds a bit confusing, but we all know what it means and it seems very appropriate.

Triumph's reputation for setting benchmarks was established with its first three-cylinder motorcycle more than a decade ago. The manufacturer went on to set the standard in the "street fighter" class with its Speed Triple, was hailed king of the retros, thanks to its modern-day Bonneville, and took the world by storm with its outrageous Rocket III, the largest-engined production bike ever built.

Now the true-Brit firm has put the cat among the pigeons once again with its phenomenal Daytona 675 middleweight sports bike. In a market that the Japanese have long dominated with their 600-cc, four-cylinder machines, the new Daytona triple promises to provoke a radical rethink.

Everything about this bike—bar its name—is different from the outgoing, four-cylinder model. The lightweight frame is so compact that it will actually fit inside that of its forebear; the engine is the first three-cylinder unit to be used in a middleweight and is physically smaller than that of any of its competitors; and the overall design gives the machine a featherlight appearance.

Triumph wants its new, baby Daytona to ooze personality in a way that its homogenized competitors simply do not manage; it wants people who own the bike to feel they are the custodians of something special— and, in truth, they are. You know this the second you hear the spine-tingling exhaust note that only a triple can produce, and that's before you've even thrown a leg over the machine and enjoyed its exceptional low-end pulling power, mid-range punch and howling top end.

Not only is this one of the neatest-looking middleweight sports bikes ever made, it is also an example of cutting-edge engineering: to save space and centralize weight, the 675 has a "stacked" gearbox positioned behind the cylinder block, and houses both the oil and the water pump inside the sump.

Minimalism, however, doesn't mean fragility, for Triumph has gone to great lengths to ensure that the 675 can be ridden hard for tens of thousands of miles. Moreover, to demonstrate its intention that the bike can, and should, be exploited on the track, it has fitted a ninety-nine-lap memory timer and created a wide range of race accessories, including lightweight, carbon-fiber parts and a competition exhaust system.

This is a middleweight sports bike in a class of its own—that is, until the others catch up.

TRIUMPH DAYTONA 675

Engine
675 cc, liquid-cooled, double-overhead-camshaft, three-cylinder, four-stroke
Power
91 kW (122 bhp) @ 12,500 rpm
Torque
72 Nm (53 ft lb) @ 11,750 rpm
Gearbox
Six-speed
Final drive
Chain
Weight
364 lb (165 kg)
Top speed
165 mph (265 km/h)

YAMAHA YZF-R1/R1SP

Engine
998 cc, liquid-cooled, double-overhead-camshaft, four-cylinder, sixteen-valve, four-stroke
Power
129 kW (173 bhp) @ 12,500 rpm
Torque
107 Nm (79 ft lb) @ 10,500 rpm
Gearbox
Six-speed
Final drive
Chain
Weight
381 lb (173 kg)
Top speed
180 mph (290 km/h)

With the launch of each new Japanese superbike, one can't help but wonder what on earth the big four manufacturers will think of next, and just how much lighter and more powerful these machines can become before they resemble nothing more than bicycles with jet engines.

The sublime levels of performance and handling that have already been attained mean that we are beginning to see less radical change and more refinement. A case in point is the new R1, which is now sniffing at the heels of Suzuki's class-leading GSX-R1000.

Engine modifications are limited to ultrafine tuning of the intake system through modified ports and shorter valve guides, which boosts power to an arm-stretching 129 kW (173 bhp). Perhaps more interesting, though, is the work that has been done on the chassis. For years we've heard how the ideal motorcycle frame should be made as stiff as possible, but now Yamaha has rewritten the rule book by building one that flexes.

The trade-off between allowing a frame to flex just enough to improve cornering and feedback to the rider, and keeping it stiff enough to hold everything together has come to be known as "rigidity balance."

With this formula in mind, Yamaha has used slimmer frame sections, reworked engine mounts, and restyled front forks to create a sharper-handling, more responsive R1 than ever before.

As well as the usual moody color schemes we have come to expect on such superbikes, the new R1 is also available in the black, yellow, and white "speed block" design that made Yamaha racers of the 1970s and 1980s so instantly recognizable on the track.

Speaking of tracks, the limited-edition R1SP is enough to set any would-be racer drooling. Based on the standard R1, the SP gets Ohlins suspension front and rear, Marchesini forged-alloy wheels, a slipper clutch, and a black-and-gold paint job. Each of the 500 examples built will bear a plaque engraved with its production number.

In *The New Motorcycle Yearbook 1*, I denounced the Yamaha R6 for being "not nearly as trendy as it once was" and said the 2005 model was nothing more than a stopgap for something far more radical—and here it is: the coolest, quickest, best-looking Japanese 600 on the market.

There's virtually nothing on this bike that is not new, from the screaming, 98-kW (131 bhp) engine, which spins eagerly up to a mind-boggling 14,500 rpm, to the ultra-aggressive bodywork and the incredibly cool, stubby side-exit exhaust system, which is made entirely from titanium.

It seems almost criminal to use this bike on the road because it is just so track-oriented—in fact, using it on the road could quickly turn you into a lawbreaker, thanks to its ability to sprint from 0 to 60 mph (0–97 km/h) in just three seconds, and to keep pulling hard until it touches 165 mph (265 km/h). And all from a machine with an engine size of just 599 cc!

This remarkable performance has been achieved thanks to a straight-air induction system, Yamaha's patented EXUP exhaust valve control, and twin-injector fueling, which combine to extend power at the top of the rev range—and it's all controlled by YCC-T (Yamaha Chip Control Throttle), the first "fly-by-wire" electronic throttle system to be used on a motorcycle.

Handling is kept taut and razor-sharp with a Deltabox frame, an ultracompact aluminum subframe, and remote adjustable suspension. And, because Yamaha expects plenty of new R6s to find their way on to racetracks, superfluous parts such as pillion footrests and number-plate mountings have been made quickly detachable.

And if the new king of the middleweights still doesn't light your fire, you could always buy one of Yamaha's official factory race kits, which include suspension-tuning parts and engine-upgrade components that boost power to the 112 kW (150 bhp) achieved by the factory-specification competition bikes. Then it really would be criminal to use the all-new R6 on the road.

YAMAHA YZF-R6

Engine
599 cc, liquid-cooled, double-overhead-camshaft, four-cylinder, sixteen-valve, four-stroke
Power
98 kW (131 bhp) @ 14,500 rpm
Torque
68 Nm (50 ft lb) @12,000 rpm
Gearbox
Six-speed
Final drive
Chain
Weight
355 lb (161 kg)
Top speed
165 mph (265 km/h)

SUPERMOTO, TRAIL, AND ENDURO

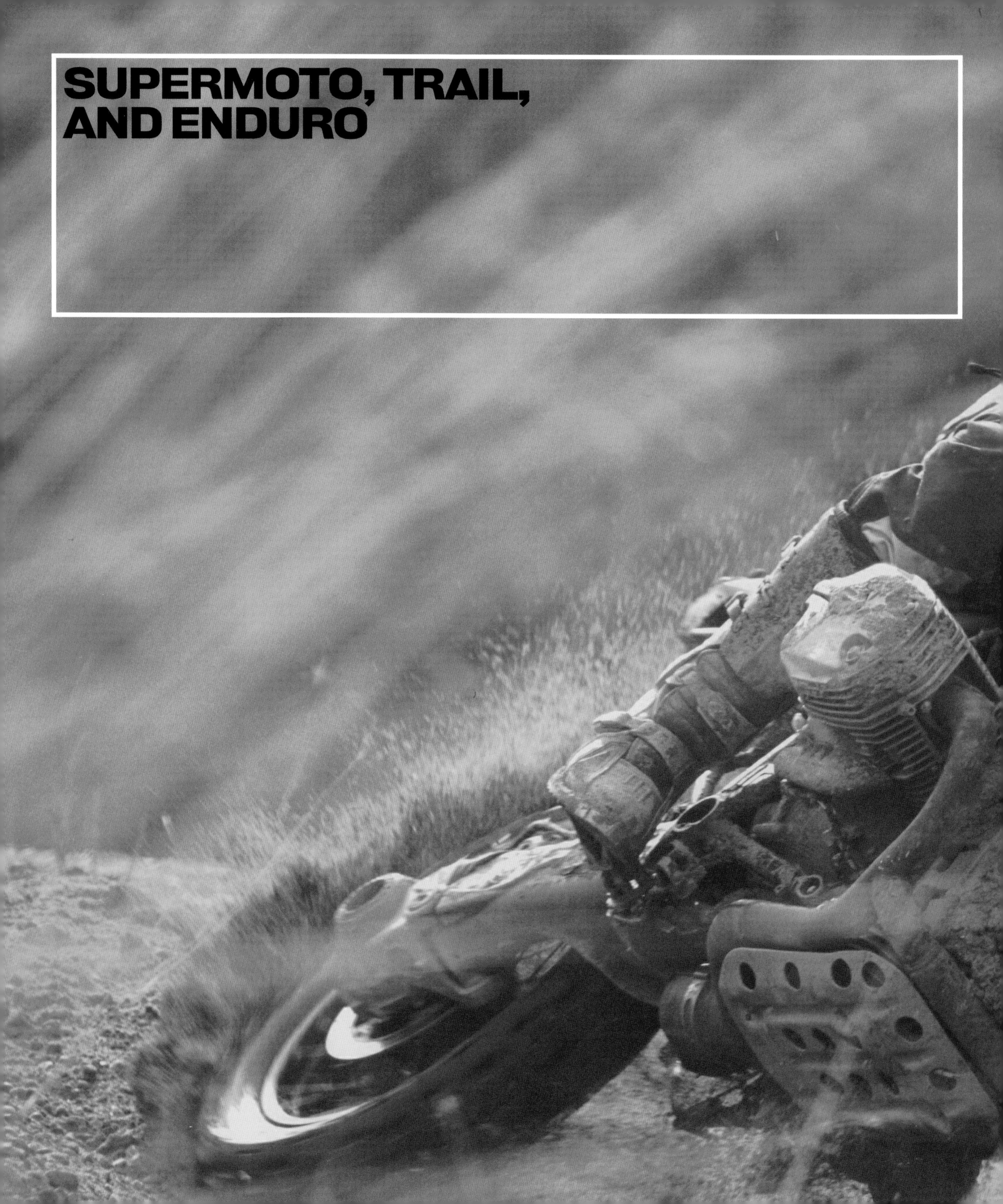

APRILIA RXV/SXV 4.5/5.5

The first edition of *The New Motorcycle Yearbook* featured Aprilia's radical SXV supermoto machine, but back then it was nothing more than a dream for road riders as it was only available as a full-blown race bike that made no concessions to highway use.

Now, however, the SXV (supermoto) and RXV (enduro) models are in full production and can be supplied with all the equipment needed to make them suitable for the road. Essentially they remain competition bikes, of course, but anyone who has already discovered the fun of riding a supermoto on the road will appreciate that the SXV has all the makings of the world's wildest two-wheeled commuter.

This is a revolutionary machine, mainly because of its powerplant, the first half-liter v-twin ever used in a motorcycle designed primarily for off-road racing. The unit is derived directly from the engine debuted by Aprilia in its 2004 championship-winning factory race bike. Although extremely light and compact, it packs a knock-out punch that its single-cylinder rivals simply cannot match. Both motorcycles make the sort of power you could have expected twenty years ago from many a 750-cc "superbike" weighing nearly twice as much.

Almost obsessive attention to detail has kept the SXV and RXV as light and slim as possible, each having minimalist plastic bodywork that is both functional and good-looking. But their real beauty lies in the gorgeous engine, cradled by a state-of-the-art aluminum trellis frame, which affords excellent access to the powerplant for maintenance without any compromise in rigidity.

A sculptured swing arm of bridge-like strength supports the bikes' back ends, which are neatly finished off with a centrally mounted, twin-pipe, underseat exhaust system that gives both machines a unique and spine-tingling voice. In the world of middleweight off-road bikes, anything else is less—for the time being, at least.

Engine
449/549 cc, liquid-cooled, 77-degree v-twin, four-stroke
Power
48 kW/52 kW (64 bhp/70 bhp) @ 13,500 rpm
Torque
Not available
Gearbox
Five-speed
Final drive
Chain
Weight
291 lb (132 kg) (est.)
Top speed
Over 100 mph (161 km/h)

For an off-road bike that separates the men from the boys, look no further than BMW's bruising HP-2. Flushed with the success of its GS range of heavyweight trail and adventure sports models, the company decided to demonstrate that its venerable air-cooled, flat-twin engine remains a practical proposition for a more competition-oriented off-roader, and the HP-2 is the result.

Minimally equipped yet still imposingly large, the bike looks as though it could ascend Everest without breaking a sweat. But the question is, who will be strong enough, confident enough and brave enough to take this monster through a quagmire, across a swollen river, or up a near-vertical hillside?

There is no doubt that the HP-2's size could be a problem in such circumstances, yet people thought exactly that when the original GS machines were launched back in 1981—until they immediately proved their worth with four wins in the Paris–Dakar desert race in quick succession.

In truth, though, many people will want to own the fully street-legal HP-2 as much for its rugged looks as for its off-road capability. The blue-painted frame, chunky tires, high-rise exhaust and small headlamp combine to give it a supercool appearance and, by stripping off the creature comforts of the standard GS model, BMW has endowed the bike with a far more exciting power-to-weight ratio.

Tweak the throttle in any of the first three gears and the front end—which is far lighter than the GS's, thanks to the replacement of the weighty Paralever suspension with standard telescopic forks—starts pawing the air just like a good enduro bike should.

The HP-2's size makes it far more comfortable than lesser machines on longer journeys, although at sustained speeds much above 70 mph (113 km/h) the lack of fairing soon makes itself felt. But, unlike most BMWs, this bike isn't really intended to be practical— it's more like the brand's latest attempt to prove that Beemers can be fun, too. And in that aim it has definitely succeeded.

Customer demand has already led to the introduction of an optional set of 17 in. (43.2 cm) street wheels and tires that turn the HP-2 into the ultimate supermoto. These are relatively straightforward to fit and remove, so the bike can be easily changed back to enduro specification for off-road use.

BMW HP-2

Engine
1170 cc, air-cooled, flat-twin, four-stroke
Power
78 kW (105 bhp) @ 7100 rpm
Torque
115 Nm (85 ft lb) @ 6200 rpm
Gearbox
Six-speed
Final drive
Shaft
Weight
386 lb (175 kg)
Top speed
125 mph (201 km/h)

CCM FT35S/ FT35R

Engine
398 cc, liquid-cooled, single-cylinder, four-stroke
Power
31 kW (42 bhp) @ 7000 rpm
Torque
39 Nm (29 ft lb) @ 5000 rpm
Gearbox
Five-speed
Final drive
Chain
Weight
287 lb (130 kg)
Top speed
90 mph (145 km/h) (est.)

The "FT" in this bike's name stands for "flat tracker," a style of motorcycle that appears to be returning to popularity after decades in the doldrums. Flat trackers were originally designed for racing on America's dirt ovals and were a variation of the speedway machines used in Europe. However, their engines were usually larger, to give greater speed on the long flat-track circuits and, importantly, they had a rear brake and rear suspension, whereas speedway bikes had neither.

The recently revived, family-run Clews Competition Motorcycles (which you can read more about on pp. 250–53) caused quite a stir at the 2005 UK motorcycle show when it unveiled the radical-looking FT35 models.

Fully road-legal, the FT35S brings flat-track styling to the street—but only for a select few. The FT35S is a limited edition, of which just 120 will be made, each with a numbered plaque on its speedo signed by the firm's founder, Alan Clews. This is truly a machine in the old tradition of British bike building—look at that hand-polished, hand-beaten aluminum fuel tank, for example—but, in terms of its componentry and engine, it is entirely up to date.

The FT35R is CCM's competition-only version of the bike and is already performing well in a new UK-based short-track race series. The R is pared down to the basics to ensure it is race-pure: no lights, no instruments, and a free-breathing, mean-sounding exhaust pipe.

CCM was in at the start of the supermoto craze back in the late 1990s, but financial troubles caused its closure before the R30 model could become fully established. Now back in the hands of its founding family and enjoying a new lease on life, the reborn British company has picked up where the old one left off and has quickly provided a brother for the 644-cc R30, the smaller-engined R35.

Fitted with high-quality suspension and brake parts and a tried-and-tested Suzuki engine from the Japanese firm's hugely popular DR-Z enduro bike, and enhanced by CCM's own unique styling, the R35 is a true dual-purpose machine that can be ridden to work and, with lights and indicators removed, raced in supermoto events on weekends.

In fact, for committed racers—and for road riders who just want to look the part and enjoy some extra wheelie power—CCM offers a big-bore kit to take the R35 up to 450 cc, a fabulous-sounding open exhaust system, rear-set race footrests, and lightweight, carbon-fiber bodywork.

The R35 is built at CCM's factory in Bolton, Lancashire, along with the 644-cc R30 dual sport and trail machines and the 404 dual sport, enduro, and trail models.

CCM R35

Engine
398 cc, liquid-cooled, single-cylinder, four-stroke
Power
31 kW (42 bhp) @ 7000 rpm
Torque
39 Nm (29 ft lb) @ 5000 rpm
Gearbox
Five-speed
Final drive
Chain
Weight
287 lb (130 kg)
Top speed
90 mph (145 km/h) (est.)

CPI SM50 SUPERMOTO

Engine
49 cc, liquid-cooled, single-cylinder, two-stroke
Power
5 kW (7 bhp) @ 10,000 rpm
Torque
Not available
Gearbox
Six-speed
Final drive
Chain
Weight
154 lb (70 kg) (est.)
Top speed
62 mph (100 km/h) (unrestricted version)

Before 1980, when some countries introduced a law restricting sixteen-year-olds to machines with a maximum speed of 30 mph (50 km/h), there was a strong market for high-performance, 50-cc sports mopeds that offered far greater street cred than conventional step-throughs with pedals.

Virtually every major manufacturer offered a hot 50, favorites being Yamaha's FS1-E, Suzuki's AP50, and the screaming, usually unreliable GT and Caballero made by the Italian firm Fantic Motor.

The introduction of performance restrictions and the arrival of the twist-and-go scooter resulted in greatly reduced interest in sports mopeds, and new ones with good performance are now few and far between.

One of the best is the latest Austrian-built CPI SM50, a scaled-down supermoto bike that rides and handles like a full-size machine and even has a decent turn of speed: its 49-cc, liquid-cooled engine produces sufficient power to push the tiny machine to 62 mph (100 km/h) or more.

Despite its diminutive size, this is a well-engineered motorcycle, with aluminum engine casings instead of the plastic normally used on small bikes, high-quality brakes and tires, a stainless-steel exhaust, and even a computerized instrument panel offering lap timing and average speed calculations, as well as the usual readouts.

With its strong performance and big-bike handling, plus the fact that it has a proper gearbox, the CPI SM50 is a far better learner machine than any twist-and-go scooter and will make any novice's progress up the motorcycle scale that much easier.

The bad news is that sixteen-year-olds in many countries will have to make do with the restricted version.

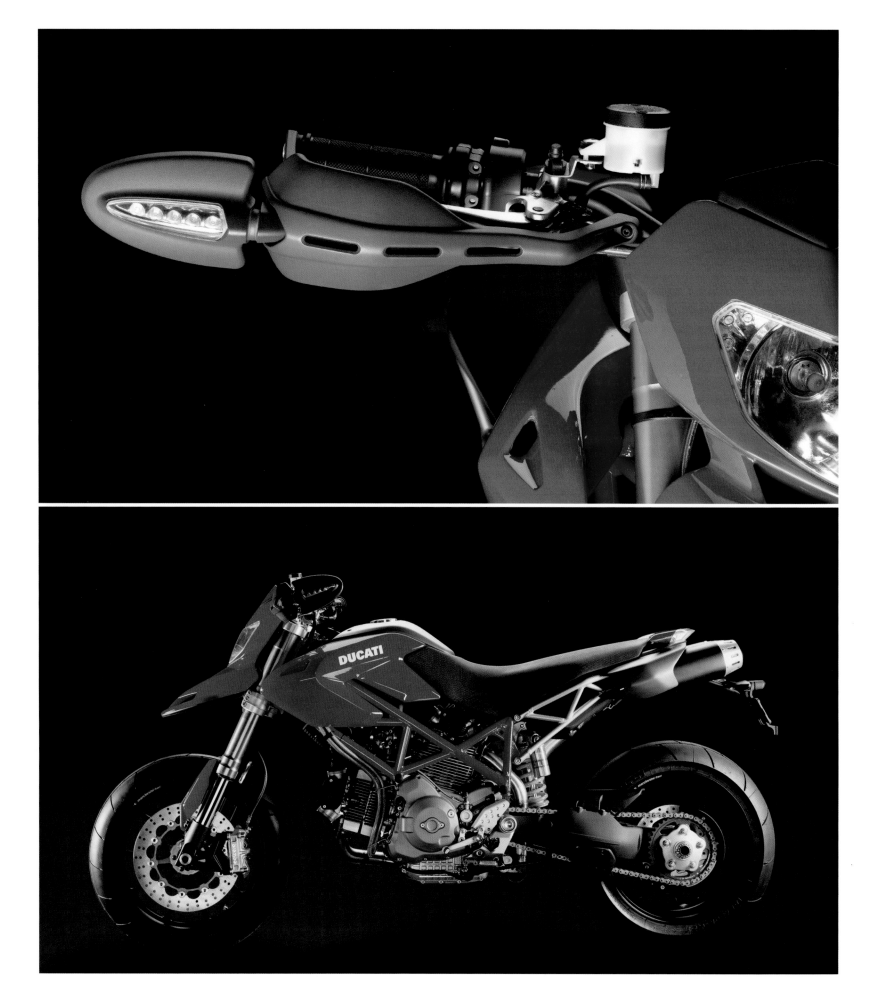

When Ducati unveiled the Hypermotard at the Milan show in November 2005, it was presented as nothing more than a concept machine, but it quickly emerged that the Italian firm was actually testing public response to one of its most radical designs of all time, with a view to putting it into production.

Unlike the 999 sports bike, which was given a unanimous thumbs down for its looks despite its excellent performance and handling, the Hypermotard was greeted with a rousing roar of approval and even won the Motorcycle Design Association's coveted award for the best-designed bike of 2005. But it was the reaction of the buying public that resulted in the concept being pushed through to the reality stage, and first deliveries are scheduled for spring 2007.

Many Ducatisti were critical of the firm's design chief, Pierre Terblanche, for creating the 999 and the peculiar-looking Multistrada, but he has regained their approval with the Hypermotard, which shows he is capable of making a cutting-edge motorcycle that looks as gorgeous as Ducati tradition demands.

As this book goes to press, it seems likely that the Hypermotard will be fitted with the tried-and-tested 1000DS "dual spark" engine used in the Multistrada and some Monster models—an ideal powerplant for a supermoto-oriented machine because of its excellent torque characteristics.

A single-sided swing arm similar to that used on Ducati's revered 916/996/998 series of sports bikes is likely to hold up the rear end, with a minimalist tailpiece being dominated by a pair of neat, angled, underseat exhausts.

The seat unit should blend seamlessly with the fuel tank for optimum rider maneuverability, and the front mudguard will be integrated into the headlamp nacelle for a truly streamlined look. The design of the rearview mirrors also demonstrates some clever thinking: integrated with the handlebar brush guards, they are designed to be folded back for track use.

A huge front disc with a radially mounted Brembo racing caliper gives the Hypermotard excellent stopping power, while state-of-the-art suspension should ensure perfect handling and "flickability."

DUCATI HYPERMOTARD

Engine
1000 cc, air-cooled, double-overhead-camshaft, twin-spark, 90-degree l-twin, four-stroke
Power
67 kW (92 bhp) @ 8000 rpm
Torque
88 Nm (65 ft lb) @ 5750 rpm
Gearbox
Six-speed
Final drive
Chain
Weight
386 lb (175 kg) (est.)
Top speed
125 mph (201 km/h) (est.)

HIGHLAND DIRT TRACKER

Highland is one of the many niche brands that have sprung up around the world over the past decade. Founded by a group of Swedish motorcycle fanatics in 1997, it produces up to two motorcycles per day at a small workshop in Skallinge in the south of the country.

Almost every component of every machine in the range is handmade, and Highland even produces its own engines, having bought the design rights for its excellent v-twin powerplants from the original manufacturer, Folan.

Highland promotes its machines as having the rideability and handling of a 500-cc, single-cylinder mount but with the thrills offered by engines of almost twice the capacity and power. Its latest model, the Dirt Tracker, takes its inspiration from the most successful competition motorcycle of all time, the Harley-Davidson XR750, which dominated US oval racing for years.

As the presence of CCM's "flat tracker" in this section of the book demonstrates, this sphere of motorcycling appears to be enjoying something of a revival, with flat-track racing becoming more and more popular in Europe.

The Highland is primarily intended as a road bike in the flat-track style, but its light weight and ultra-powerful v-twin engine give it all the credentials it needs to be an effective competition machine. Indeed, an American race team is already successfully campaigning Highland bikes on the dirt ovals.

Engine
936 cc, liquid-cooled, double-overhead-camshaft, 60 degree v-twin, four-stroke
Power
63 kW (85 bhp) @ 6000 rpm
Torque
104 Nm (77 ft lb) @ 4000 rpm
Gearbox
Six-speed
Final drive
Chain
Weight
364 lb (165 kg)
Top speed
Over 120 mph (193 km/h)

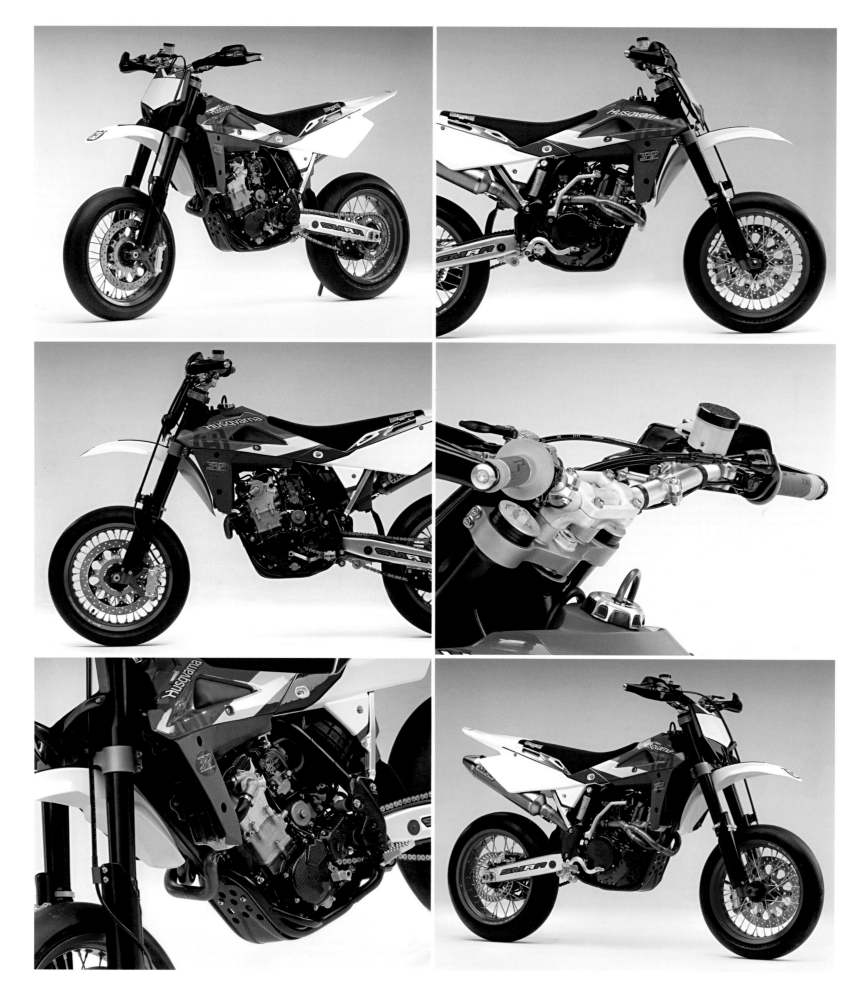

Street-legal supermoto bikes may have become the coolest way to beat urban gridlock, but the Swedish firm Husqvarna will never lose sight of its competition heritage. Founded in 1903, it started out making single-cylinder and v-twin road bikes and race machines, but after the Second World War the company established an unrivaled reputation for its motocross and long-distance trials machines.

This led to competition bikes becoming Husqvarna's mainstay, and the brand was favored by many celebrated dirt-bike racers, among them the actor and motorcycle fanatic Steve McQueen. That competition-oriented philosophy survives today and is epitomized by the SM450RR, an uncompromising supermoto for track use only. In creating it, Husqvarna hopes to help buyers realize every racer's dream of unpacking a new bike, taking it straight on to the track—and winning. The SM450RR certainly has the pedigree: it is based directly on the factory bike that took the laurels in the 2005 world championship and is designed to be competitive straight from the crate.

A shortened swing arm makes for ultraquick handling, the engine is a full-blown motocross unit, and the free-flow exhaust system is made from titanium, front to back. A slipper clutch reduces rear wheel lock-up during the hard downshifts that supermoto demands, and Brembo radially mounted brakes are fitted front and back, with weight kept to a minimum through the use of carbon fiber for parts such as engine covers, the chain guard, and the front mudguard brace.

To emphasize the race-ready appeal of the bike, each SM450RR comes complete with a paddock stand, spare sprockets to alter the gearing, and spacers to adjust the steering angle for slower or quicker turning, depending on how twisty the track is.

HUSQVARNA SM450RR

Engine
449 cc, liquid-cooled, double-overhead-camshaft, single-cylinder, four-valve, four-stroke
Power
41 kW (55 bhp) @ 7000 rpm (est.)
Torque
Not available
Gearbox
Five-speed
Final drive
Chain
Weight
258 lb (117 kg)
Top speed
90 mph (145 km/h), depending on gearing

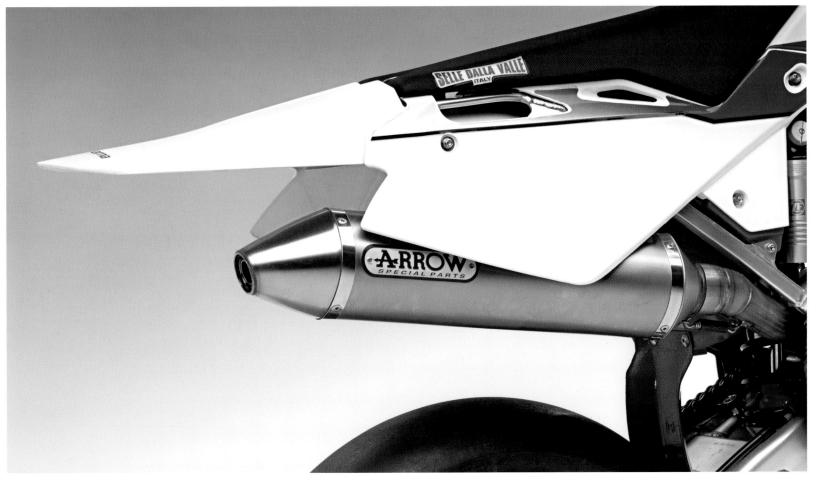

KTM 950 SUPER ENDURO R

Engine
942 cc, liquid-cooled, double-overhead-camshaft, 75-degree v-twin, four-stroke
Power
73 kW (98 bhp) @ 8500 rpm
Torque
95 Nm (70 ft lb) @ 6500 rpm
Gearbox
Six-speed
Final drive
Chain
Weight
408 lb (185 kg)
Top speed
120 mph (193 km/h) (est.), depending on gearing

Derived from the ultracapable 950 Adventure overlanding machine, KTM's new Super Enduro R is just that: a superbike for off-road racing. But this is no machine for the dirt-bike novice, combining as it does a hugely powerful 942-cc engine with a seat height of 33.8 in. (86 cm).

In keeping with its competition status, the Super Enduro R has been slimmed down by almost 33 lb (15 kg) from its adventure sports cousin, making it easier to turn and manoeuvre off-road and slightly less of a strain to pick out of a muddy ditch when everything goes wrong.

Equipment has been minimalized, too. A smaller-capacity fuel tank holding 13 liters (3.4 US gallons) and a narrower seat help make the bike less cumbersome; the frontal area is greatly reduced; and instrumentation is restricted to the basic speedometer and trip setup required for competitive enduro racing, although there will be plenty of owners who use their Super Enduros for straightforward green-laning and perhaps even commuting.

The second use would rather waste the KTM's race-bred componentry, which includes taut, long-travel White Power suspension front and rear, ultralight wheels, and a tough aluminum bash plate.

The heart of the machine, however, is the superlative 942-cc, carburetor-fed, v-twin engine, which remains the lightest powerplant of its type fitted to a current production motorcycle.

The "MH" in this little motorcycle's name stands for "Moto Hispania," a long-established manufacturer based in Seville that has drawn on Spain's history of designing great off-road bikes to produce a small but perfectly formed machine that not only looks good but also is highly capable.

Power comes from a top-quality, 50-cc, water-cooled Minarelli two-stroke engine equipped with a six-speed gearbox. The small capacity reflects the fact that this is an entry-level machine aimed at the youth market but, in unrestricted form, the Furia Max will reach around 50 mph (80 km/h). That might sound a little tame, but on tight, twisting, muddy trails this bike would be preferable to many machines of ten times its engine capacity precisely because it is so small, light and maneuverable.

Its fixtures and fittings would not look out of place on a more uncompromising competition bike, either. The Paioli suspension and hefty beam frame are up to handling substantial jumps, the twin disc brakes are more than adequate for the bike's light weight, and the ergonomic tank-seat tail unit not only is handsome but also allows the rider excellent freedom of movement.

More committed off-road riders can opt for a "ProRace" package that adds 1.5-in. (38 mm) "upside down" forks, an adjustable rear shock absorber, "breaking wave" brake discs, handlebar brush guards, and a less restrictive exhaust system.

As well as the enduro-styled model, the Furia Max is available in "supermotard" guise with road wheels and tires, a larger front brake disc and an electric starter.

MH FURIA MAX

Engine
50 cc, liquid-cooled, single-cylinder, two-stroke
Power
4 kW (5 bhp) @ 7000 rpm (est.)
Torque
Not available
Gearbox
Six-speed
Final drive
Chain
Weight
209 lb (95 kg); supermotard 214 lb (97 kg)
Top speed
30 mph (48 km/h); derestricted 55 mph (88 km/h)

TERRA MODENA 198

Engine
449 cc, liquid-cooled, gear-driven double-overhead-camshaft, single-cylinder, four-stroke
Power
43 kW (58 bhp) @ 8000 rpm (est.)
Torque
Not available
Gearbox
Six-speed, cassette type
Final drive
Chain
Weight
265 lb (120 kg)
Top speed
100 mph (161 km/h)

Readers of *The New Motorcycle Yearbook 1* may have spotted the Terra Modena in the Supermoto section. At that time the handful of SX2 bikes that the tiny Italian manufacturer had completed were mainly for track use, although some were fitted with lights to show their road-going potential.

Now, however, the production version is here, and it's called the 198; "1" indicates the number of cylinders and "98" the size of the cylinder bore in millimeters. This is one of the most expensive supermoto bikes on the market, but Terra Modena can justify the price by the development work that has gone into the specially designed engine and the amount of top-quality cycle parts with which the 198 is equipped.

The 450-cc, single-cylinder powerplant was developed by Pierro Ferrari of the legendary Italian sports-car manufacturer; brakes are by race specialists Brembo; Ohlins provides the suspension; Marchesini supplies the wheels; and, to ensure that every Terra Modena that leaves the factory will stick to the road like glue, Dunlop Sportmax tires come as standard.

Apart from the red of the engine block, no paint is used on the bike, which has carbon-fiber and Kevlar bodywork and an aluminum and titanium frame. And there are no optional extras because, as Terra Modena's founder Dario Calzavara says: "Its standard equipment is already all that can currently be desired in a motorbike."

The original SX2's single exhaust pipe has been replaced by a custom-designed twin silencer developed by performance exhaust specialists HPE Tubi Style, which, combined with Terra Modena's special airbox (complete with airfoils based on the 1975 312T Formula One car) ensures superefficient combustion.

WHITE KNUCKLE 300

In some ways trail bikes have gotten too big for their boots: too much engine, too much weight, and too much sophistication are not what a rider needs when trying to pick a path across a swollen river or scramble up a mountain track. The unusually named White Knuckle, however, is everything a good trail bike used to be: light, lithe, tough, and torquey. And, being a Chinese-built machine, it is something of a bargain, since it is priced at the same level as most Japanese 125s.

What you get for your money is an engine based on that from the discontinued Suzuki DR350 (one of the best midsize trail bikes ever), contemporary "upside down" front forks with lots of travel, alloy wheel rims with chunky, off-road tires, a digital gear position indicator, and a sturdy parcel rack.

Admittedly the frame is an old-fashioned steel-tube affair and the standard of finish may not match that of the bike's more expensive rivals, but this is still a proper trail bike for budget money.

Riders in the US have been able to buy a version of the White Knuckle for off-road use only since 2005, but this street-legal, fully homologated model is expected to attract European trail riders, entry-level enduro competitors and, of course, crosstown commuters.

A road wheel kit allowing the White Knuckle to be converted into a supermoto-style machine is about to become available. Also in the pipeline is an upgraded version featuring a 450-cc engine and a lightweight beam chassis.

Engine
249 cc, overhead-camshaft, single-cylinder, four-stroke
Power
19 kW (25 bhp) @ 8500 rpm
Torque
25 Nm (18 ft lb) @ 7000 rpm
Gearbox
Five-speed
Final drive
Chain
Weight
265 lb (120 kg)
Top speed
75 mph (121 km/h)

CRUISERS

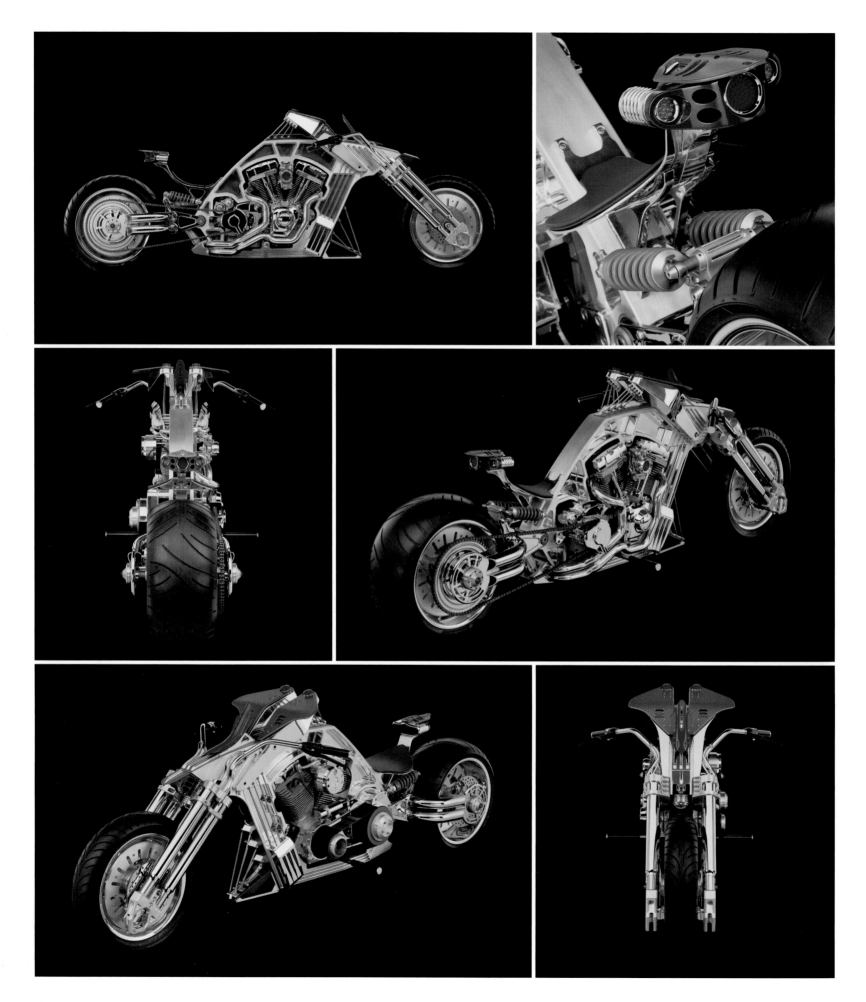

Readers of the American edition of *The New Motorcycle Yearbook 1* may recall that the jacket was illustrated with images of a radical-looking custom-built motorcycle: the Dreamcraft DCS-001. Now engineer Larry Nagel and designer Paul Yang (see pp. 242–45) have taken their wild imaginations a step further and produced the DCS-002 Rapture, a machine that is already regarded by some critics as the most remarkable motorcycle ever built.

Looking like it has been wheeled out of an alien reconnaissance vehicle to scout around Earth, the Rapture comprises a mass of gleaming chrome and polished alloy. The fanatical collector who commissioned it specified a machine that would look like a vehicle inspired by the films *Star Wars* and *Mad Max*!

It bristles with extraordinary features, from the massive quad fork front end, which is held to the frame by a handmade spindle around 3 in. (7.5 cm) thick, to the frame itself. From a solid, 900-lb (408 kg) block of T6 aircraft-grade aluminium, no less than 700 lb (318 kg) of metal was removed to create the indestructible-looking frame, the top section of which houses twin fuel tanks, mounted high to conceal the rider's body from view.

The exhaust system is another highlight of the design: waste gases exit through a pair of ceramic-coated pipes that connect with a tubular rear swing arm fitted with eight semicircular outlet holes. Racing-car cantilever-suspension technology has enabled the shock absorbers to be horizontally mounted behind the swing arm's pivot point.

Nagel and Yang have designed the Rapture not just as a showstopper, but as a totally rideable motorcycle, although they would probably be the first to admit that it is more likely to end up as the centerpiece of a collection of contemporary art or design than as anyone's everyday means of transport.

DREAMCRAFT DCS-002 RAPTURE

Engine
1449 cc, Harley-Davidson, v-twin, four-stroke
Power
60 kW (80 bhp) @ 5000 rpm (est.)
Torque
109 Nm (80 ft lb) @ 3400 rpm (est.)
Gearbox
Six-speed
Final drive
Chain
Weight
780 lb (354 kg)
Top speed
110 mph (177 km/h) (est.)

HARLEY-DAVIDSON FLSTI HERITAGE SOFTAIL

It takes a true Harley aficionado to know at a glance the differences between the many different model names—the Softail, the Springer, the Fat Boy, the Dyna, and so on.

What marks out a Softail, however, is the fact that it has a concealed rear suspension system as opposed to the conventional, twin-shock setup used on other Harley-Davidsons, a feature instigated in 1984.

The FLSTI Heritage Softail was dropped from the range a while ago but is now back by popular demand. This is the Harley on which more dreams of riding into the sunset with no agenda are based than any other: a wide, plush saddle, comfortable footboards, a relaxed riding position, and, at the heart of it all, a rigid-mounted, 1449-cc, twin-camshaft engine to effortlessly pull you along.

This year, other models in the Softail range, the FXSTI Standard and the minimalist FXSTBI Night Train, get new 7.9-in. (20 cm) wide rear tires for a meaner cruiser look.

Engine
1449 cc, air-cooled, double-overhead-camshaft, v-twin, four-stroke
Power
45 kW (60 bhp) @ 5500 rpm
Torque
106 Nm (78 ft lb) @ 4000 rpm
Gearbox
Six-speed
Final drive
Belt
Weight
677 lb (307 kg)
Top speed
110 mph (177 km/h)

Described by Harley-Davidson as an "undressed dresser," this is a touring bike for those who want comfort and carrying capacity without the myriad extras found on the "full dress" Ultra Classic Electra Glide.

Wind protection is provided by a top-half headlamp fairing of a design that was probably conceived around 1955, while solid, color-matched panniers offer adequate carrying capacity. The retro look is completed by a pair of straight exhaust pipes exiting on either side of the machine.

One concession to modern touring you will find on the Street Glide is a state-of-the art Harman Kardon sound system that pumps out 80 watts of power through a four-speaker system.

HARLEY-DAVIDSON FLHCI STREET GLIDE

Engine
1449 cc, air-cooled, double-overhead-camshaft, v-twin, four-stroke
Power
45 kW (60 bhp) @ 5500 rpm
Torque
109 Nm (80 ft lb) @ 3400 rpm
Gearbox
Six-speed
Final drive
Belt
Weight
732 lb (332 kg)
Top speed
110 mph (177 km/h)

HARLEY-DAVIDSON FXDBI DYNA STREET BOB

Engine
1449 cc, air-cooled, double-overhead-camshaft, v-twin, four-stroke
Power
45 kW (60 bhp) @ 5500 rpm
Torque
106 Nm (78 ft lb) @ 4000 rpm
Gearbox
Six-speed
Final drive
Belt
Weight
639 lb (290 kg)
Top speed
110 mph (177 km/h)

From a distance this new Dyna could be a home-built special created by a 1960s rebel, but get up close and you'll see that the Street Bob is Harley-Davidson's latest take on the original "factory custom" bikes it first offered in 1971 with the Super Glide.

The most obvious feature of the Street Bob is those impossibly high "ape hanger" handlebars, which are a good pointer to the fact that this is a machine for unashamed posing. Indeed, anyone intending to ride a Bob for longer than five minutes at anything over 62 mph (100 km/h) would do well to book a session with their physiotherapist before taking to the road.

The minimalist, outlaw theme is continued in the single saddle, the tiny, round headlamp, and the stretched frame with its steeply raked steering head that is designed to create the perfect laid-back cruiser look.

In fact, Harley-Davidson claims to have faithfully followed postwar "bobber" culture (which "bobbed" motorcycles by cutting off all unnecessary components), leaving behind only those parts required by law.

Despite its extreme length, the Street Bob is an adequate handler, thanks to substantial front forks and a wide swing arm that houses a fat rear tire—entirely necessary when you are running a 1449-cc v-twin that pumps out an impressive 106 Nm (78 ft lb) of torque at a lowly 4000 rpm.

As a machine for low-speed cruising with the wind in your face and "Born to be Wild" in your headphones, there are few production bikes to match the Street Bob, especially when finished in moody "Black Denim" matt paintwork, which is designed to patinate with age like a pair of favorite jeans.

Rather tired of its image as a producer of old-fashioned, somewhat slow cruisers, Harley-Davidson established its Custom Vehicles Operation (CVO) in 1999 in order to offer a limited-edition "super breed" of hand-tuned machines.

The V-Rod, with its water-cooled, Porsche-designed engine, already shows that production Harleys can be fast, but the new Night Rod, Street Rod, and Screamin' Eagle versions from CVO take the bikes to another level.

Engines can be bored out to 1250 cc from the standard 1131 cc, trick intake cams fitted, and cylinder heads gas-flowed, all of which potentially increases horsepower by up to 10% and gives torque a useful boost.

The Night Rod is intended to look menacing and it does, with its black frame, black engine, blacked-out mirrors, and chrome, straight-through exhaust pipes complemented by aluminum disc wheels.

The Street Rod improves on the normal V-Rod's cornering ability by virtue of its mid-mounted footrests and controls, shorter handlebar risers, and a taller seat that has been designed to move the rider into a more aggressive position for rapid bend-swinging. Also, the wheelbase has been reduced by altering the fork angle to 32 degrees.

CVO's ultimate road-going performance offering (as opposed to the dragstrip-only V-Rod Destroyer, described pp. 230–31) is the Screamin' Eagle V-Rod, which has a tuned and bored engine and comes in an eye-catching orange-and-black-pearl paint finish.

HARLEY-DAVIDSON VRSCD NIGHT ROD/ VRSCR STREET ROD/VRSCSE SCREAMIN' EAGLE V-ROD

Engine
VRSCD and VRSCR 1130 cc; VRSCSE 1250 cc; liquid-cooled, v-twin, four-stroke
Power
VRSCD and VRSCR 88 kW (119 bhp) @ 8250 rpm; VRSCSE 95 kW (127 bhp) @ 8500 rpm
Torque
VRSCD and VRSCR 108 Nm (80 ft lb); VRSCSE 137 Nm (101 ft lb) @ 7000 rpm
Gearbox
Five-speed
Final drive
Belt
Weight
606 lb (275 kg)
Top speed
Over 140 mph (225 km/h)

HERO PLUTO

Cruiser bikes have monster engines, huge back tires, elongated frames, and trucklike proportions—but all that's no use if you want to cruise without having gained your motorcycle license. It is for "learner cruisers" that machines such as the new Hero Pluto exist: a motorcycle powered by a lowly, 125-cc, single-cylinder engine fitted in a raked-out frame with pullback handlebars and a stepped seat.

Oddly, the cruiser configuration actually works better on a lightweight motorcycle than it does on a full-size or even oversize one: the Pluto's ergonomics make it easy to maneuver in traffic and more comfortable to ride than a conventionally styled commuter bike.

This machine even has "cruiser pegs" and remote brake and gear controls that force the rider into a laid-back position. Just like a baby Harley, it incorporates a tank-mounted instrument pod and a neat little tail pad for the passenger.

The engineering is basic and the finish merely adequate—that chrome will need some serious care if it is to maintain its lustre through a winter in the northern hemisphere—but the little Pluto is both excellent value for money and the most accessible route there is into cruiser territory. And the low seat height makes it great for women and shorter male riders, too.

Engine
124 cc, air-cooled, overhead-camshaft, single-cylinder, four-stroke
Power
7 kW (10 bhp) @ 8500 rpm
Torque
9 Nm (7 ft lb) @ 7500 rpm
Gearbox
Five-speed
Final drive
Chain
Weight
333 lb (151 kg)
Top speed
70 mph (113 km/h)

The renaissance of motorcycling that has taken place during the past decade or so has forced all the major manufacturers to think hard about producing the widest possible range of machines that will appeal to new riders.

Cruisers were at one time very much considered a category of motorcycle that people grew into after sampling street, sport, and touring machines, and finding that none quite fitted their personality. With the VN900, however, Kawasaki is hoping to tempt new license holders straight into cruiser culture with a bike that has been designed to look as though it is powered by one of the huge engines that have become *de rigueur* in the field.

The thinking behind the VN900 is that the mere thought of riding a motorcycle with an engine of 1500 cc or more will put novices off, even if such a big-bore engine is tuned to be as soft as a pussycat. Kawasaki's gambit is to offer a machine that boasts the physical presence of its VN2000 but has a sub-one-liter engine so as to give less experienced riders the opportunity to own a cruiser that isn't such a bruiser.

A superfat rear tire gives the bike traffic-light kudos, the large-capacity fuel tank allows a decent touring range, and the final drive employs the clean, convenient belt method. To damp down the type of vibrations usually inherent in a big v-twin, Kawasaki has fitted the engine with lightweight, boltless con rods and made it refined and quiet with water cooling. A comfortable stepped seat provides adequate space for a passenger and the full cruiser look is completed by slash-cut stacked exhausts, tank-mounted instrumentation, and the obligatory polished-chrome air filter mounted between the cylinders.

KAWASAKI VN900

Engine
903 cc, liquid-cooled, v-twin, four-stroke
Power
52 kW (70 bhp) @ 5000 rpm (est.)
Torque
Not available
Gearbox
Five-speed
Final drive
Belt
Weight
507 lb (230 kg) (est.)
Top speed
110 mph (177 km/h)

MOTO GUZZI CALIFORNIA VINTAGE

Engine
1064 cc, overhead-valve, v-twin, four-stroke
Power
55 kW (74 bhp) @ 6400 rpm
Torque
55 Nm (41 ft lb) @ 5000 rpm
Gearbox
Five-speed
Final drive
Shaft
Weight
580 lb (263 kg)
Top speed
120 mph (193 km/h)

It was difficult to decide whether to include Moto Guzzi's new California Vintage in the Cruisers, Tourers, or Retro section of this book because it fits perfectly into all three categories.

Everything about the bike, from its two-tone seat to its pinstriped tank, and from its analog instruments to its fat, wire-spoked wheels, screams of the 1970s, so much so that any fortysomething male who remembers the Guzzis ridden by the California Highway Patrol in the TV show CHiPs is bound to be transported back in time.

But this bike is a serious contemporary tourer, too: check out the fabulous saddlebags, comfortable footboards, auxiliary lights, stainless-steel-framed screen and practical crash bars—all pulled along by a modernized version of the air-cooled, push-rod twin-cylinder unit that powered those original machines.

Taken directly from the latest Breva 1100, the engine offers thoroughly modern performance, thanks to Magneti Marelli fuel injection and twin-plug cylinder heads, while emissions are taken care of by catalytic converters hidden inside a pair of mufflers that are excellent imitations of those used on the 1970s California.

Anyone who owned one of the originals will be pleased to hear that the electrical system and switchgear has also been brought right up to date, for in the old days Guzzi engines would run forever but the wiring looms used to self-destruct.

Motorcycle manufacturers are seldom shy about blowing their own trumpet, and Suzuki's latest boast is the piston size of its awesome-looking new Intruder cruiser. "Ladies and gentlemen, meet the motorcycle with the largest reciprocating engine pistons being used on Earth in any production motorcycle or passenger car," proclaims the sales brochure.

There is certainly no doubt that each 891.5-cc cylinder bore is large enough to sink a fist into, and the slugs that fill them look as though they have been borrowed from a giant truck. Despite the resulting raw power, Suzuki has tamed the beast by making its 54-degree engine configuration run as smoothly as a 90-degree setup, by using offset crank pins to provide what it describes as "perfect primary balance."

The Intruder is definitely a handsome beast, its swooping headlamp cowl and flowing lines recalling Honda's Valkyrie Rune limited-production cruiser. More crucially, though, Suzuki has used technology from its supersports GSX-R1000, such as the fuel-injection system and the radially mounted brakes, to enhance the bike's performance.

But what the company appears most proud of is the Intruder's 9.4-in. (240 mm) section rear tire, the largest ever used on a Suzuki motorcycle. Buyers who don't relish the thought of spending all their savings on rubber should, perhaps, keep burnouts to a minimum.

SUZUKI M1800R INTRUDER

Engine
1783 cc, liquid-cooled, double-overhead-camshaft, v-twin, four-stroke
Power
Not available
Torque
Not available
Gearbox
Five-speed
Final drive
Chain
Weight
694 lb (315 kg)
Top speed
120 mph (193 km/h) (est.)

TRIUMPH ROCKET III CLASSIC

Engine
2294 cc, liquid-cooled, double-overhead-camshaft, in-line three-cylinder, twelve-valve
Power
104 kW (140 bhp) @ 5750 rpm
Torque
199 Nm (147 ft lb) @ 2500 rpm
Gearbox
Five-speed
Final drive
Shaft
Weight
705 lb (320 kg)
Top speed
135 mph (217 km/h)

Although launched as recently as 2005, Triumph's Rocket III cruiser can justifiably be called a classic: that title was guaranteed almost as soon as it hit the street, with the largest engine ever fitted to a production motorcycle.

But the "Classic" tag on this latest version refers to the fact that this is a Rocket for laid-back cruising. With its massive torque output and monstrous power, the "standard" model does tend to bring out the drag racer in even the most staid of motorcyclists, but the Classic has been given a more relaxed character, with rider footboards, pullback handlebars and a supercomfortable touring seat.

The options list runs to no fewer than forty-five items, ranging from panniers to fly screens, sissy bars, and chrome additions, while the Classic also benefits from a custom paint job in either black with a sunset-red infill or cherry red with a white infill—in either case the gold coachlining is hand-applied at the Triumph factory.

With all that torque at the end of the twist grip, the Rocket III makes a great basis for a long-distance, easygoing tourer, and the Classic, when equipped with panniers, screen, and a few other optional extras, is likely to become the bike of choice for cruiser riders who want to do a little bit more than just be seen on main streets.

Victory is a young American motorcycle maker founded in 1998, but it has already established itself as America's "second" cruiser bike maker after Harley-Davidson. It says something for Victory's credibility in the market that custom-bike guru Arlen Ness has agreed to lend his revered name to a new, limited-edition series of Vegas Jackpot models, when it was he who was called upon by the firm's owner, Polaris, to design the original motorcycle range.

One of the trademarks of every Victory machine is the high-quality finish, which makes the bikes look individually handbuilt, and in the case of the Ness editions, this is pretty close to the truth. Featuring the type of extreme custom styling for which Ness is famous, the Vegas Jackpot specials have radical paint schemes, signed side covers, and hand-stitched seats created by the famed custom upholsterer Danny Gray.

The wheels are seven-spoke works of art hewn from billet aluminum, and even the mirrors and handlebar grips have been given special Ness detailing, the grips featuring an engraved diamond pattern.

Just like the standard bikes, the Ness Signature models are fitted with a 1634-cc engine that produces lots of low-down torque and feeds through to a six-speed gearbox in which top is effectively an overdrive ratio for relaxed high-speed cruising.

VICTORY VEGAS JACKPOT "NESS SIGNATURE SERIES"

Engine
1634 cc, air- and oil-cooled, fuel-injected, single-overhead-camshaft, 50-degree v-twin, four-stroke
Power
63 kW (85 bhp)
Torque
136 Nm (100 ft lb) @ 3500 rpm
Gearbox
Six-speed overdrive
Final drive
Belt
Weight
644 lb (292 kg)
Top speed
120 mph (193 km/h)

YAMAHA XV1900 MIDNIGHT STAR

If you can't beat them, join them. That seems to have become the philosophy among Japanese motorcycle manufacturers after they were forced to admit that Harley-Davidson got it right the first time when it began putting v-twin engines into cruiser bikes.

Yamaha's latest attempt at a Harley clone is the XV1900 Midnight Star, a large-scale cruiser with awesome presence. Its fuel-injected, catalytic-converter-equipped engine has nothing like the character or sound of a Harley (although a certain degree of what Yamaha calls "feel good vibes" have been built in), but boy, does it pull.

The firm's own EXUP exhaust control system has been used to great effect in order to provide the machine with that essential cruiser characteristic: waves of torque at the merest tweak of the twist grip, making it a really impressive straight-line performer. In fact, if there's a torquier motorcycle out there I'd very much like to hear about it. It even outgrunts the 2.3-liter Triumph Rocket III.

In an attempt to create an individual finish, Yamaha has added hand-polished clutch and cylinder head covers and a neat set of twelve-spoke aluminum wheels. And just cast an eye over those chromed push-rod tubes running up the outside of each cylinder: they're for real, as this is a good, old-fashioned overhead-valve engine.

Engine
1854 cc, air-cooled, overhead-valve, v-twin, four-stroke
Power
75 kW (100 bhp) @ 4250 rpm
Torque
167 Nm (123 ft lb) @ 2500 rpm
Gearbox
Five-speed
Final drive
Belt
Weight
705 lb (320 kg)
Top speed
120 mph (193 km/h) (est.)

ADVENTURE
SPORTS

The standard for adventure sports motorcycles was set when BMW launched the original R1150 GS Adventure back in 2002. An off-the-shelf production bike built and equipped for serious overlanding had never before been available, and the fact that BMW decided to produce one demonstrates the seismic shift that has recently occurred in motorcycling.

The German manufacturer spotted a niche for a well-designed go-anywhere, long-distance tourer well before anyone else. It saw that motorcycling was being embraced by the cash-rich, time-rich professional who was bored with conventional vacations and wanted a little more adventure in life.

Actor Ewan McGregor and traveling companion Charley Boorman gave the Adventure a massive marketing boost by choosing it for their now-legendary Long Way Round tour (see p. 17), with interest peaking just in time for the customers to start lining up for this latest, even better model.

The new Adventure is based on the brilliantly competent R1200 GS big trail bike and bristles with equipment and features previously only available as special equipment or accessories, such as a 32-liter (8 US gallons) fuel tank that gives a potential range of 465 miles (290 km), protector hoops for the tank and engine and adjustable brake and gear levers to complement the extra-wide footrests.

This bike is also considerably lighter than the outgoing Adventure—useful when it's lying on its side in a sand dune—and offers a 17% increase in torque, which could also be useful for getting out of the same dune once you've picked it up.

Like the R1200 S, it is equipped with single-wire CAN-bus technology that powers an Info-Flatscreen. And, mindful that this bike has excellent on-road cruising capability, BMW has improved rider protection by fitting an extra-large, angle-adjustable windshield.

Other practical touches include a sturdy, stainless-steel luggage rack, extra suspension travel, and bar-mounted hand protectors. A high-output alternator enables the electrical system to cope with a variety of available extras, such as heated clothing, auxiliary lighting, and an onboard computer system that monitors ambient temperature, fuel range, average fuel consumption, and average speed as well as low oil level and ice risk.

Also developed for the Adventure is an entirely new aluminum luggage set comprising top case and panniers that have a combined capacity of 112 liters (3.9 cu. ft) and come supplied with waterproof inner bags.

So, if you're ready to pack it all in and set off around the world, don't forget to take one of these with you.

BMW R1200 GS ADVENTURE

Engine
1170 cc, air-cooled, flat-twin, eight-valve, four-stroke
Power
74 kW (100 bhp) @ 7000 rpm
Torque
115 Nm (85 ft lb) @ 5500 rpm
Gearbox
Six-speed
Final drive
Shaft
Weight
492 lb (223 kg)
Top speed
125 mph (201 km/h)

BUELL ULYSSES

Engine
1203 cc, air-, oil-, and fan-cooled,
45-degree v-twin, four-stroke
Power
75 kW (100 bhp) @ 6600 rpm
Torque
110 Nm (81 ft lb) @ 6000 rpm
Gearbox
Five-speed
Final drive
Belt
Weight
425 lb (193 kg)
Top speed
115 mph (185 km/h)

There's no denying that a lightweight motorcycle with a low center of gravity and a grunty, large-capacity v-twin engine makes a great on-road/off-road adventure sports machine, and this is Erik Buell's take on the idea. The Ulysses is perhaps the most radical creation yet to emerge from the production line of the Harley-Davidson-owned company. It's the sort of machine Mad Max should have been riding.

Powered by the Buell-tuned, Harley-built Thunderstorm engine, the Ulysses carries its fuel in the frame and its oil in the swing arm, just as the Firebolt road bike does. But there the similarity ends, as the off-roader gets a wheelbase 2 in. (5 cm) longer to make it less skittish on the dirt and high, wide handlebars for extra leverage.

The handlebars incorporate useful brush guards that offer protection against everything from thorny branches to wind blast and, of course, other vehicles' wing mirrors during the rush-hour commute.

One of the most practical features of the Ulysses—and a clever piece of design—is its so-called "triple tail." This simple folding platform can be used as a passenger backrest, an extended luggage carrier mounted over the bike's tailpiece, or as a way of converting the pillion seat into a stable load platform.

The only question marks surrounding the machine's suitability for off-road use lie in its vulnerable underbelly exhaust system and the large, rim-mounted brake disc, which could be prone to rock damage when the bike is ridden fast over rough terrain. The traditional Buell belt drive has also been retained, but this is expected to perform equally well in all conditions.

To make the Ulysses a sales contender in the face of more established adventure sports bikes such as those from BMW and KTM, Buell also offers a range of color-matched luggage and a quickly detachable GPS navigator.

Back in 1985 Yamaha launched a single-cylinder trail bike called the XT600 Tenere, a road-legal machine based on the manufacturer's successful Paris–Dakar desert racers. Its main difference from the production XT600 was the addition of a large-capacity fuel tank that made the model particularly popular with fans of long-distance touring.

Despite having a single-cylinder engine of modest power, the Tenere proved to be a brilliant go-anywhere vehicle, and its tall seat height and long-travel suspension meant it could be loaded to the gunwales with gear and still remain comfortable.

It is the Tenere's unexpected success all those years ago that led to the production of machines such as KTM's 640 Adventure. This is the bike for people who don't need the top-end performance of the powerful, one-liter Adventure and appreciate the benefits of having a lighter, easier-to-handle machine that is a far more practical proposition in tricky, off-road situations.

The new 640 Adventure has enough grunt to deliver a rider, passenger, and touring gear to the edge of the wilderness and, when they get there, the torque, agility, and handling to, in KTM's words, "track through sands or weave along jungle trails."

As you would expect of any KTM, build quality is excellent and components are all of top quality. One particularly nice touch is the use of a hydraulically operated clutch, a feature seldom found on mid-capacity trail bikes but one that makes a great deal of sense. For not only is a hydraulic clutch lighter and smoother to use while pootling around off-road, it is also maintenance-free, so no more snapped cables to leave you stranded miles from civilization.

KTM 640 ADVENTURE

Engine
625 cc, overhead-camshaft, single-cylinder, four-stroke
Power
40 kW (54 bhp) @ 8200 rpm
Torque
71 Nm (52 ft lb) @ 8200 rpm
Gearbox
Five-speed
Final drive
Chain
Weight
348 lb (158 kg)
Top speed
100 mph (161 km/h)

KTM 990 ADVENTURE

The popularity of adventure sports motorcycles shows little sign of abating, so it's no surprise that KTM has upgraded its highly capable Adventure model to ensure it can still compete against the quality competition from other manufacturers, most notably BMW.

Thanks to the maker's long-standing reputation for producing top-quality off-road bikes, the KTM Adventure tends to be the natural choice of overlanding riders with dirt-bike experience who want a machine that is slightly more oriented towards the rough stuff than the BMW—hence the "travel enduro" tag that the bike has been given by its Austrian makers.

The trade-off for achieving this advantage is that the KTM is perhaps slightly less refined than its German rival and considerably more biased toward off-road use than Japanese adventure sports machines—although it remains perfectly capable of eating up the distances on the open road.

At first glance the new Adventure doesn't appear to be much different from the old one, but it is at the bike's heart that changes have occurred, for it has been fitted with the larger, 999-cc, fuel-injected LC8 engine first used by KTM on its Super Duke street bike. This replaces the old model's heavier, less powerful, carburetor-fed, 950-cc unit.

The new Adventure also follows BMW's lead in being equipped with antilock brakes—which can, of course, be deactivated at times when the bike is being used off-road. And, knowing that most overland trips usually result in a spill or two, KTM has incorporated crash protectors into the lower sections of the fairing and constructed the 22-litre (6 US gallons) fuel tank from unbreakable nylon.

Two versions of the Adventure are available: the standard model and the more focused S variant, which features longer suspension travel and a special "Dakar" paint scheme in homage to the famously grueling annual desert race.

KTM has developed its own range of robust, high-capacity luggage especially for the Adventure range, and specialist overlanding firms such as Touratech offer myriad aftermarket extras with which to personalize the machines and make them into even more formidable continent-crossers than they are already.

Engine
999 cc, liquid-cooled, double-overhead-camshaft, 75-degree v-twin, eight-valve, four-stroke
Power
72 kW (97 bhp) @ 8500 rpm
Torque
95 Nm (70 ft lb) @ 6500 rpm
Gearbox
Six-speed
Final drive
Chain
Weight
439 lb (199 kg)
Top speed
115 mph (185 km/h)

Japan's offerings in the adventure sports category are not quite as hard-core as those of its European rivals, but there are still plenty of riders who believe that when it comes to value for money, reliability, finish, and longevity, the products of the "big four" are hard to beat.

It is at these people that the V-Strom range—named after a Bavarian river—is aimed, and adventure sports bikes such as the Suzuki are proving so popular for long-distance work that it might not be too long before they are outselling purpose-built touring bikes.

With their commanding riding positions, lazy yet inexhaustible engines, and superb comfort, machines such as the V-Strom can be ridden all day at respectably high speeds without inducing fatigue.

In a bid to attract even more hard-riding tourists, Suzuki is now offering V-Stroms with all the equipment needed to set off on an adventure straight from the showroom floor. The 1000-cc Grand Touring model comes equipped with a 48-liter (1.7 cu. ft) top case, panniers, a center stand, heated grips, and hand guards, while its smaller-engined cousin, the Touring, has to make do without the panniers but gets everything else.

The Touring is aimed more at newly qualified riders but, in its nontouring guise, it has proved to be ultrapopular as a commuter bike, thanks to the proven reliability of its SV650-derived engine, its low fuel consumption, and its generally inexpensive running costs—plus, of course, that comfort factor it shares with the bigger machine.

SUZUKI V-STROM DL 1000 GRAND TOURING/DL 650 TOURING

Engine
Grand Touring 996 cc; Touring 645 cc; fuel-injected, double-overhead-camshaft, 90-degree v-twin, four-stroke
Power
Grand Touring 73 kW (98 bhp) @ 7600 rpm; Touring 50 kW (67 bhp) @ 9000 rpm
Torque
Grand Touring 101 Nm (74 ft lb) @ 6400 rpm; Touring 60 Nm (44 ft lb) @ 6400 rpm
Gearbox
Six-speed
Final drive
Chain
Weight
Grand Touring 459 lb (208 kg); Touring 419 lb (190 kg)
Top speed
Grand Touring 145 mph (233 km/h); Touring 120 mph (193 km/h)

SPORTS
TOURERS

For more than half a century, BMW has been synonymous with twin-cylinder motorcycles, but its F800 series is a radical departure from the norm because it is powered by a vertically inclined engine rather than the horizontally opposed ones traditionally used by the make.

BMW commissioned the Austrian engineering firm Bombardier-Rotax to design and supply the all-new powerplant. This features water cooling, fuel injection, a high compression ratio of 12:1, and an eight-valve cylinder head with a combustion chamber based on that of the ultrapowerful K1200 S four-cylinder unit.

All this results in a healthy output of 63 kW (85 bhp), which, combined with the F800's light weight, gives the bike a similar performance to the R1200 "boxer" twin models. Mid-range torque is particularly strong, which makes the machine a relaxed long-distance road-eater and provides it with excellent hill-climbing ability and roll-on acceleration. That high compression ratio is useful on a tourer, too, because it makes for excellent fuel economy and so greater distances between fill-ups.

Look closely at the F800 and you'll notice certain features common to BMW's F650 trail-style, single-cylinder machine: the side-mounted fuel filler for the underseat fuel tank, for example, as well as the traditional telescopic front forks, the single-sided swing arm, and the belt final drive.

Although much more advanced and refined, the F800 is similar in concept and characteristics to Yamaha's TRX 850 of the 1990s, which was the Japanese firm's attempt at making a Ducati-styled sports bike. Nowadays, though, you need a power output much greater than this machine's to make it into the pure sports-bike category, so both the F800 S and the F800 ST can be classed as sports tourers.

The S version is, however, a little more rakish, with its shorter screen, sportier riding position, and lack of a lower fairing. The ST comes equipped with a set of specially designed aluminum panniers and mounting brackets. Also available is BMW's traditional list of touring options, such as antilock brakes, heated grips, auxiliary electrical sockets, and an onboard computer.

This machine marks the start of a new era in the middleweight sports-touring category.

BMW F800 S/ST

Engine
798 cc, liquid-cooled, double-overhead-camshaft, parallel-twin, four-valve, four-stroke
Power
63 kW (85 bhp) @ 8000 rpm
Torque
80 Nm (59 ft lb) @ 5800 rpm
Gearbox
Six-speed
Final drive
Belt
Weight
454 lb (206 kg)
Top speed
130 mph (209 km/h)

DUCATI ST3s ABS

Ducati's ST (Sport Touring) range has been around for a decade, which might lead some to think that it's in need of a radical overhaul or even complete replacement. Ducati thinks otherwise, however, for the ST series has a loyal following among a particular type of rider: those who want the sound, feel, and sense of a real v-twin motorcycle, rather than the sanitized, homogenized, whisper-quiet tourers produced by the Japanese.

With that in mind, the Bologna-based firm has allowed the ST to gently evolve over the years, and the latest result of this is the ST3s ABS. The "3" refers to the number of valves per cylinder and the "s" denotes that the bike has been treated to a suspension package more closely related to a sports bike than a sports tourer.

Distinguishable by its new-design, five-spoke wheel rims, the ST3s ABS also gets fully adjustable "upside down" Showa forks with a special, antifriction "TiN" coating similar to that used on Ducati's pure sports bikes. A top-quality Ohlins suspension unit with remote adjustment takes care of the rear end and new, quick-release body panels have been designed with the intention of reducing servicing times and therefore costs.

Elsewhere the bike retains such useful touring features as fully adjustable handlebars, electronically controlled headlamp alignment, and exhaust mufflers that can be raised for sports riding or lowered to accommodate the custom-made pannier system.

Engine
992 cc, l-twin, three-valve, four-stroke
Power
79 kW (106 bhp) @ 8750 rpm
Torque
103 Nm (76 ft lb) @ 7250 rpm
Gearbox
Six-speed
Final drive
Chain
Weight
448 lb (203 kg)
Top speed
145 mph (233 km/h)

The fact that the ZZ-R1400 is large, with a comfortable riding position and plenty of room for a passenger and luggage, makes it a sports tourer, but it is in the "sports" department that this bike really gets noticed, for it is probably the fastest production motorcycle of all time.

The many fans of the old ZZR models, bikes with 600-cc, 1100-cc, and 1200-cc engines, mourned when production came to an end, but it wasn't long before Kawasaki was promising a stunning replacement. And it has kept its word.

"The Big K" has long had a reputation for building the fastest bikes on the block, thanks to machines such as the Z1 of the 1970s, the GPZ 900 of the 1980s, the ZZ-R1100 of the 1990s, and, most recently, the ZX-12R.

The ZZ-R1400 is, however, officially the fastest road bike Kawasaki has ever made. In standard form it is restricted to 186 mph (300 km/h) to honour an unwritten agreement among the major manufacturers on speed limitation but, in derestricted form, the bike is said to be easily capable of breaking the 200-mph (320 km/h) barrier.

Yet this machine's true brilliance lies in the fact that its monstrous power output can be delivered in a gentle trickle or in a g-force-inducing torrent with equal ease. Weaving through traffic on minimal throttle is as simple a matter as sending the world into reverse at warp speed with a less conservative twist of the wrist.

Acceleration is immensely strong throughout the rev range, but when the tachometer needle swings to the 6000-rpm mark, the ZZ-R releases every bit of its

481 kW (197 bhp) through the heavy-duty drive chain and on to the 7.5-in. (190 mm) section rear tire—with predictable results.

Massively powerful brakes derived from those used on the ZX-10R hypersports machine are capable of pulling the ZZ-R up briskly from very high speeds, and an overengineered light alloy frame prevents the monstrous torque of the engine from twisting things out of shape.

If you're a tourist in a hurry, this is the bike for you.

KAWASAKI ZZ-R1400

Engine
1352 cc, liquid-cooled, double-overhead-camshaft, four-cylinder, four-stroke
Power
481 kW (197 bhp) @ 12,000 rpm
Torque
155 Nm (114 ft lb) @ 8000 rpm
Gearbox
Six-speed
Final drive
Chain
Weight
474 lb (215 kg)
Top speed
186 mph (300 km/h) (restricted)

STREET, NAKED, AND MUSCLE

It is common practice to create a 'naked' bike by starting with a super-sports machine, removing the full fairing, converting the race-style riding position to a 'sit-up-and-beg' configuration, and significantly detuning the engine.

With its new Tuono R, Aprilia appears to have done all the above except for the last. This machine is basically a Mille R with high handlebars and, as a result, it's completely crazy. To be fair, its power output is some 4 kW (5 bhp) less than its race-replica cousin's and Aprilia claims to have improved mid-range torque, but the average rider will barely notice the difference.

The 60-degree v-twin engine provides enormous thrust and will lift the front wheel off the throttle in the first two gears and, with judicious clutch slipping, in third as well. The bike's wide handlebars make it far more comfortable to ride in traffic, but the race-bred nature of the Mille R is still there, and that means a rather snatchy low-speed power delivery, suspension that feels rigid unless it's really being made to work, and a steering lock that is impractically narrow for filtering through dense traffic.

But a one-liter v-twin that punches out 99 kW (133 bhp) was probably never intended for daily commuting anyway, and it is on snaking minor roads that the Tuono R really comes alive, squirting from bend to bend on controllable waves of torque and flicking from left to right like a machine half its size.

This sweet handling is attributable to top-quality, fully adjustable suspension components (just like those on the Mille, of course), including 1.7-in. (43 mm) Showa upside-down front forks, an aluminum "double banana" swing arm and the maker's own APS (Aprilia Progressive System) rising rate suspension linkage attached to a Sachs hydraulic monoshock. The brakes are Brembo racing units.

APRILIA TUONO R

Engine
997 cc, liquid-cooled, double-overhead-camshaft, 60-degree v-twin, eight-valve, four-stroke
Power
99 kW (133 bhp) @ 9500 rpm
Torque
102 Nm (75 ft lb) @ 8750 rpm
Gearbox
Six-speed
Final drive
Chain
Weight
408 lb (185 kg)
Top speed
150 mph (241 km/h) (est.)

BENELLI TRE-K

The TRE-K could appear in the Adventure Sports section on the grounds that Benelli is pitching it against machines such as the Multistrada and Triumph Tiger; but, apart from the upright, trail-style looks, this seems the complete street bike.

Just as the Multistrada melded two very distinct types of motorcycle when it was launched in 2003, so the TRE-K takes a road-bike engine and combines it with a chassis that gives a commanding, upright riding position and sharp handling but, realistically, no off-road capability.

There is no doubt, however, that this new Benelli incorporates the typically gorgeous looks for which the Italian manufacturer is renowned. The rear light has been molded around the single underseat muffler to create an understated rear end, while the bikini fairing envelops the front of the fuel tank to give a purposeful aerodynamic look.

To ensure the bike has lots of torque and tractable power for both town riding and roaring along twisty back roads, the TRE-K's engine is a detuned Tornado sports-bike unit. The frame is taller and longer than that of the Tornado, too, so handling is still excellent—just not quite as sharp or quick as that of its sportier brother.

Engine
1130 cc, double-overhead-camshaft, three-cylinder, four-stroke
Power
92 kW (123 bhp) @ 9000 rpm
Torque
114 Nm (84 ft lb) @ 6250 rpm
Gearbox
Six-speed
Final drive
Chain
Weight
441 lb (200 kg) (est.)
Top speed
145 mph (233 km/h)

Taking the fairing off a fancy sports bike to create an equally fancy naked is all the rage nowadays, and that is just what Bimota has done with its delicious new Delirio.

Based on the exotic DB5, the Delirio is a short, stubby bike in the true streetfighter tradition. The DB5's distinctively shaped headlamp gets a cut-down version of the sports bike's upper fairing, and the rounded exhausts of the original are replaced on the Delirio by a pair of end cans more in keeping with Bimota's trademark angular styling.

The low-volume Italian manufacturer has been sourcing its engines from Ducati of late, and the Delirio comes equipped with the 1000-cc, twin-spark engine used in Ducati's Multistrada. It produces a little more than 67 kW (90 bhp), which is quite lowly compared with the 89 kW (120 bhp), 97 kW (130 bhp), and even 104 kW (140 bhp) of some of the Delirio's competitors. But performance is all about power-to-weight ratio, and that is where this bike scores. Aluminum frame parts and other lightweight components mean it tips the scales at less than 331 lb (150 kg)—far lighter than rival machines such as the Aprilia Tuono and Buell Lightning.

But in terms of price the Delirio is much less of a bargain: following the Bimota tradition, this is one of the most expensive nakeds on the market, costing around $27,600. That's almost half as much again as MV Agusta's similarly exotic Brutale; but then exclusivity never did come cheap.

BIMOTA DELIRIO

Engine
992 cc, air-cooled, fuel-injected, l-twin, four-stroke
Power
69 kW (92 bhp) @ 7750 rpm
Torque
56 Nm (41 ft lb) @ 5750 rpm
Gearbox
Six-speed
Final drive
Chain
Weight
326 lb (148 kg) (est.)
Top speed
130 mph (209 km/h) (est.)

BUELL LIGHTNING XB12S LONG

Engine
1203 cc, air-cooled, v-twin, four-stroke
Power
75 kW (100 bhp) @ 6600 rpm
Torque
110 Nm (81 ft lb) @ 6000 rpm
Gearbox
Five-speed
Final drive
Belt
Weight
399 lb (181 kg)
Top speed
125 mph (201 km/h)

My first ride on a Buell Lightning nearly left me feeling extremely foolish: eager to make the most of the bike's tuned Thunderstorm v-twin, I immediately cracked open the throttle and was almost deposited on the deck as a great gob of torque instantly hoisted the tiny machine up to the vertical. It was a firm reminder that motorcycles are only as dangerous as the person controlling them, but there is no doubt that the ultrashort chassis of the standard Lightning does make the bike a bit skittish.

It is partly for this reason that the American manufacturer has introduced the XB12S Long, a lengthened and heightened version of the Lightning. The change has been brought about by the simple expedient of using the frame from the Buell Ulysses, featured in the Adventure Sports section (pp. 124–25). That gives the Long a seat height of 30.5 in. (77.5 cm) (0.4 in./10 mm higher than standard) and a wheelbase that is more than 2 in. (5 cm) longer.

These increased dimensions not only make the bike more comfortable for distance work, but have enabled the fitting of a larger fuel tank, holding 16.7 liters (4.4 US gallons), which adds 30 miles (48 km) to its touring range.

Mechanically, the Long benefits from an improved gearbox for smoother shifts and it retains all the trick bits with which Buell is synonymous, such as the rim-mounted front brake disc, the underslung exhaust system, and fuel and oil tanks that are incorporated into the frame and swing arm respectively.

Although it is perhaps not such a fast-turning and "flickable" machine as the shorter XB12S, the Long still handles like a dream and benefits from additional high-speed stability and greater comfort, particularly over rough surfaces. Pillion passengers will certainly prefer it—not least because they will now have a chance of staying on when the front end starts to head skyward.

Making good motorcycles seems to be getting easier, partly because CAD-CAM (computer-aided design and manufacture) equipment is far less expensive and more accessible than ever. This is good news for the motorcycle industry, because it has enabled niche makers to enter the fray with interesting new products, fresh designs and sometimes quite radical ideas. True, they don't always work, but at least this way motorcycles will be prevented from heading down the road of homogenization that cars seem to be following.

The Vun, or "One," began life as a oneshot project bike designed and built by a trio of friends, but it received such a positive response from the public that it was decided to put it into limited production.

Powered by a hopped-up version of the 650-cc, single-cylinder engine used in BMW's F650 GS trail/commuter bike, the Vun promises sharp handling thanks to its low center of gravity, and frame concepts derived from those used by the late New Zealand designer John Britten. Britten, who built a short series of legendary race bikes based around his own hypertuned v-twin engines, was a close friend of Roberto Crepaldi, who founded CR and S along with fellow bike fan Giorgi Sarti, the firm's president.

With its spoked wheels, slim swing arm, and minimalist back end, the Vun has an almost delicate appearance and is impressively light. It features an underslung, midmounted muffler in the style of Buell, and nice details such as "breaking wave" brake discs with radial calipers and a smattering of carbon fiber.

CR and S—the name stands for "Café Racers and Superbikes"—will offer the Vun with three engine options: a restricted version for newly qualified riders, a standard 40-kW (54 bhp) version and a tuned 51-kW (68 bhp) model.

CR AND S VUN

Engine
652 cc, overhead-camshaft, twin-spark, single-cylinder, four-stroke
Power
25 kW/40 kW (33 bhp/54 bhp) @ 7000 rpm or 51 kW (68 bhp) @ 7500 rpm
Torque
59 Nm (43 ft lb) @ 5000 rpm or 65 Nm (48 ft lb) @ 7000 rpm
Gearbox
Five-speed
Final drive
Chain
Weight
298 lb (135 kg)
Top speed
85 mph (135 km/h) or 110 mph (177 km/h)

DUCATI MONSTER 695

Engine
695 cc, air-cooled, l-twin, two-valve, four-stroke
Power
54 kW (73 bhp) @ 8500 rpm
Torque
61 Nm (45 ft lb) @ 6750 rpm
Gearbox
Six-speed
Final drive
Chain
Weight
370 lb (168 kg)
Top speed
120 mph (193 km/h)

Time was when a 750-cc motorcycle was considered a "superbike," but now Ducati's basic Monster has grown to 695 cc and yet it's still looked upon as an ideal entry-level machine for newly qualified riders.

The new 695 is a replacement for the "little" 620-cc Monster, which has been around since 2001. It offers a healthy power boost—up more than 7 kW (10 bhp)—that makes it the most powerful motorcycle per cc ever produced by Ducati. The engine tweaks are said to have made the bike even more tractable and easy to ride in town.

Meanwhile, the machine's aesthetic appeal has been freshened up with some subtle cosmetic detailing. Electrical wires and cabling have been artfully hidden to provide an uncluttered view of the sculptural engine and frame layout; components such as the front forks, swing arm, and clutch covers have been given a dose of black paint; and the color of the Ducati logo has changed from muted silver to a more vibrant white. The bike's Italian heritage is also proudly displayed through the addition of the red, white, and green *tricolore* on the two side panels.

The yellow paintwork option available on the outgoing 620 has been dropped, but the 695 is available in a red frame version with either red or gloss-black paintwork or with a black frame and matt-black paintwork.

The Monster must be one of the most evergreen motorcycle designs of all time: the first incarnation of Migual Galluzi's iconic machine appeared in 1993, yet the model remains the mainstay of the Ducati brand. Part of the reason for this success is that the bike offers mass appeal: girls love it and boys love it; if you're a newly qualified rider, there is the tame 25-kW (33 bhp), 620-cc model mentioned elsewhere in this section; then come various capacity options and engine types, and now, at the top of the Monster tree, you will find the fire-breathing S4Rs.

This is the hottest Monster ever because it packs the Testastretta ("narrow head") engine originally designed for the 999 superbike, endowing the S4R with 97 kW (130 bhp), scorching acceleration and endless potential for wheelies.

The new model also gets the 999's Y-spoke wheels, its top-grade Ohlins front forks, an upgraded 999 rear shock absorber, and race-standard, radially mounted Brembo brakes. Those twin exhausts are also special, because they are made by the Italian tuning house Termignoni and fitted with carbon heat shields to match the S4R's special timing belt covers.

To complete its sporty appearance, this monstrous Monster is fitted with a neat headlamp fairing and a glass-fiber seat cowl that can be removed to reveal a small but adequate pillion seat. White paintwork and red racing stripes boost the cool factor.

DUCATI MONSTER S4Rs

Engine
998 cc, overhead-camshaft, l-twin, eight-valve, four-stroke
Power
97 kW (130 bhp) @ 9500 rpm
Torque
104 Nm (77 ft lb) @ 7500 rpm
Gearbox
Six-speed
Final drive
Chain
Weight
390 lb (177 kg)
Top speed
150 mph (241 km/h)

DUCATI MONSTER S2R 800 33 BHP

Engine
803 cc, air-cooled, v-twin, four-valve, four-stroke
Power
25 kW (33 bhp) @ 5500 rpm
Torque
73 Nm (54 ft lb) @ 6500 rpm
Gearbox
Five-speed
Final drive
Chain
Weight
381 lb (173 kg)
Top speed
100 mph (161 km/h)

Probably more novice and would-be motorcyclists aspire to own a Ducati than any other brand, but the very fact that the lineup is epitomized by large-capacity, high-performance machines that mostly cost considerably more than their Japanese rivals, means that aspiring is as far as most of them ever get.

The most accessible Ducati has always been the entry-level 600, which grew first to 620 cc and, most recently, the 695-cc version featured elsewhere in this section. Now, however, the Italian firm has introduced a variation of its 803-cc S2R model that is limited to produce just 25 kW (33 bhp), as compared with the 57 kW (77 bhp) of the standard machine.

This means that newly qualified riders in countries that restrict the inexperienced to machines of 33 bhp or less, can now own, ride and savour a big-bore Ducati that, after a year's probationary period, can easily be derestricted and returned to its full power specification. The restrictor kit is nothing more complex than a device that limits the amount of available throttle opening. Otherwise the S2R is just that: an S2R, with the same twin-cam, high-level exhaust system, same bikini fairing, and same great Ducati handling.

It is a clever move by Ducati and one that might just prevent new riders from cutting their teeth on Japanese machinery and staying loyal to it without ever sampling the sophisticated offerings of Italy's best-loved motorcycle manufacturer. What is more, the price is quite reasonable, at just a little above the cost of a Japanese 600-cc street bike.

"The most practical, most desirable piece of art in their collection" is how Ecosse founder Donald Atchison believes owners of these most exclusive of motorcycles will come to regard them.

Atchison established Ecosse in 2001 as a supplier of limited-production, custom street bikes for the discerning buyer with plenty of cash: the top-of-the-range Ti model costs $139,800 and even the "entry-level" version costs almost $50,000.

For that you get an entirely handbuilt machine constructed from exotic materials and parts that are individually made at the Ecosse Moto Works in Denver, Colorado—even the dynamically balanced and blueprinted engines are built in-house, as is the chassis, which, on the Ti version, is created from titanium—a world first in the motorcycle industry.

When you pay this sort of money for a motorcycle you can demand virtually any specification you like: engine sizes from 1640 cc to 1966 cc are available, and you can have your own personal message engraved into the handlebar clamps, and choose any color and finish you desire.

No two Heretics are identical, but all abound with neat features such as starter buttons that double as oil warning lamps, programmable tachometers that can be equipped with quarter-mile (0.4 km) timers, and instruments with adjustable needle colors.

Carbon fiber and Kevlar are used extensively on the bodywork—there is no plastic on an Ecosse—and every piece is hand-finished to perfection, while the wheels (which can also be made from carbon fiber if so desired) are made to the same pattern as the brake discs.

The Heretic is undeniably expensive, but Atchison says buyers are really getting three motorcycles in one because each machine comes with multiadjustable footrests and handlebars that allow the bike to be quickly transformed from a road racer to a cruiser to a dragster.

In any mode, performance is guaranteed from the top engine option, which produces up to 190 Nm (140 ft lb) of torque at less than 3000 rpm, suspension that is custom-built for Ecosse by Ohlins and massive, six-piston radial brakes that are said to be better than those used on Grand Prix machines.

ECOSSE HERETIC

Engine
(Ti optimum model) 1966 cc, air-cooled, v-twin, four-stroke
Power
104 kW (140 bhp) @ 5800 rpm (est.)
Torque
190 Nm (140 ft lb) @ 2800 rpm (est.)
Gearbox
Six-speed
Final drive
Chain
Weight
450 lb (204 kg)
Top speed
150 mph (241 km/h) (est.)

HONDA CBF250

Honda was the brand responsible for putting the world on two wheels and, for all its supersports machines and globe-shrinking tourers, it never forgets the importance of workaday motorcycles. Its most famous machine is, of course, the step-through Cub, more than fifty million examples of which have been sold since it was launched in the 1960s.

The CBF250 is a couple of steps up from the ubiquitous Cub, being a no-nonsense quarter-liter machine that is unashamedly designed for going from A to B as conveniently as possible. There is nothing flash or fancy about this bike, but buy one and maintain it properly and it will give reliable, economical service for many years to come. This I can vouch for as the owner of a 1970s version of the venerable parallel twin that runs as well today as it did thirty years ago. Hondas come with reliability built in.

The latest, single-cylinder CBF250 comes with a large-diameter front-brake disc and low-maintenance drum at the rear, a useful 16-liter (4.2 US gallons) fuel tank sufficient for at least 200 miles (320 km) of town riding, and wide, low-profile tires for greater comfort and traction. One of the few concessions to luxury is the inclusion of a balancer shaft to cut down on engine vibration but apart from that and a wide, comfortable seat, this is back-to-basics motorcycling at its best.

Engine
250 cc, double-overhead-camshaft, single-cylinder, four-valve, four-stroke
Power
16 kW (21 bhp) @ 8000 rpm
Torque
22 Nm (16 ft lb) @ 6000 rpm
Gearbox
Six-speed
Final drive
Chain
Weight
304 lb (138 kg)
Top speed
90 mph (145 km/h)

Honda's new CBF1000 is what many people will refer to as a "real" motorcycle: a big, powerful engine, lots of presence on the road, and the capacity to cruise all day, carrying a passenger and luggage without breaking a sweat.

It makes do without the myriad accoutrements of a Gold Wing or the plastic cladding of a sports bike, it won't be the fastest thing around a racetrack and its appearance is more traditional than cutting edge—and that is what makes it the epitome of traditional one-liter motorcycling.

This is Honda's latest product in its "Just Fit" program of motorcycles that are designed for ease of use and versatility. The CBF1000 is intended to be as simple and undemanding to ride as, say, the entry-level Hornet 600, and Honda has gone to great lengths to make the machine a suitable choice for every type of rider.

The seat can be fixed in three different positions, the handlebars can be given a 0.4-in. (10 mm) forward offset for taller riders and the screen of the wind-tunnel-tested fairing can be adjusted to a variety of heights.

In addition the engineers have ensured that the CBF is as unintimidating as possible by making what is really a large motorcycle seem compact and manageable, and by retuning the engine, which is borrowed directly from the latest CBR1000RR Fireblade supersports machine.

Now, instead of being an explosive, high-revving beast, the unit provides manageable power and torque at the low revs where it is most needed in real-world riding, so endowing the bike with excellent highway constancy and making it docile in traffic. The added benefit of the engine's light state of tune is that it is understressed and so should last for a huge mileage.

An impressive pair of stainless-steel, oval-shaped mufflers has been designed to give the CBF a healthy growl worthy of its bruising personality, while from a practical point of view Honda has produced a useful range of accessories, including 35-liter (1.2 cu. ft) and 45-liter (1.6 cu. ft) top boxes and 29-liter (1 cu. ft) and 33-liter (1.2 cu. ft) pannier bags. Carbon-fibre-style instrument covers are also available, as well as a color-matched engine cover set, handlebar knuckle protectors, a rear wheel hugger, and a seat cowl.

The bike can also be ordered with a version of Honda's combined ABS.

HONDA CBF1000

Engine
998 cc, double-overhead-camshaft, four-cylinder, sixteen-valve, four-stroke
Power
72 kW (97 bhp) @ 8000 rpm
Torque
97 Nm (71 ft lb) @ 6500 rpm
Gearbox
Six-speed
Final drive
Chain
Weight
485 lb (220 kg) (ABS version 503 lb/228 kg)
Top speed
140 mph (225 km/h)

ITALJET GRIFON

Italjet was founded in 1966 by Leopoldo Tartarini, at that time a well-known motorcycle racer in his native Italy. The first bikes used CZ and Triumph engines, but the make became best known for its 50-cc children's bikes, a series of middleweight road bikes (including one called the Grifon), and several successful trials models.

During the 1990s Italjet rode the crest of the scooter wave, introducing its radical Dragster, which remains a cult model. In 2002, however, the firm went bust, but was revived three years later by Massimo Tartarini, Leopoldo's son.

The first model in the reborn Italjet range is the tidy-looking Grifon, which is made in the popular v-twin street-bike mold. It uses a 650-cc engine built by the huge Chinese company Hyosung. Although it looks stylish, there is nothing particularly exotic about the Grifon, and this is intentional: the use of a simple steel frame and adequate running gear keeps production costs low and may give the firm a chance to establish itself.

Another model, the Bazooka, is also offered. Mechanically the same as the Grifon, it has sportier bodywork and cast-alloy wheels.

Engine
647 cc, liquid-cooled, 90-degree v-twin, four-stroke
Power
59 kW (79 bhp) @ 9000 rpm
Torque
68 Nm (50 ft lb) @ 7500 rpm
Gearbox
Six-speed
Final drive
Chain
Weight
418 lb (190 kg) (est.)
Top speed
110 mph (177 km/h) (est.)

Kawasaki's old ER-5 was not the world's most exciting motorcycle in terms of looks or performance, but it was loved by newly qualified riders, hardened commuters and dispatch riders for its unbeatable combination of reliability, value for money, and versatility. With the ER-6, however, the company has moved the middleweight parallel-twin machine into the twenty-first century by giving it decidedly funky looks and increasing the engine's power without compromising on the bike's capabilities as a practical all-round vehicle.

High handlebars and a deep seat give the ER-6 a comfortable riding position for both town and distance work, but above all the bike has been designed to be light and responsive, features that make it much more exciting than its power or size suggest. It is designed to inspire confidence and to introduce novices to the fun of biking, and it succeeds in both aims.

Despite offering displacement of 150 cc more than the ER-5, the new machine has an exceptionally compact engine and the overall look has been conceived with the intention of making the bike appear at once lithe, agile, and reassuring. The lightweight frame is made from a latticework of slim tubes and the lay-down rear shock absorber leaves plenty of free space, adding to the impression of lightness; curling exhaust downpipes double back on themselves to end in a trick-looking, midmounted muffler. Kawasaki's design team has even gone to work on the footpegs: they are carried on a single sculpted aluminum bracket that also incorporates those for the passenger.

The bulbous plastic protrusions of the N (for "naked") version of the bike are intended to lend it a tough, streetfighter look, but the lack of fairing makes it rather hard work to ride at sustained highway speeds; as a result, Kawasaki also offers the option of the F (for "faired") at a slightly higher price. In either case you get a lot of bike for your money.

KAWASAKI ER-6 N/F

Engine
649 cc, double-overhead-camshaft, parallel-twin, eight-valve, four-stroke
Power
53 kW (72 bhp) @ 7000 rpm
Torque
66 Nm (49 ft lb) @ 7000 rpm
Gearbox
Six-speed
Final drive
Chain
Weight
N 384 lb (174 kg); F 393 lb (178 kg)
Top speed
125 mph (201 km/h)

MORINI CORSARO 9 1/2

Engine
1187 cc, liquid-cooled, double-overhead-camshaft, 87-degree v-twin, four-stroke
Power
97 kW (130 bhp) @ 8500 rpm (claimed)
Torque
123 Nm (91 ft lb) @ 6500 rpm
Gearbox
Six-speed
Final drive
Chain
Weight
437 lb (198 kg)
Top speed
148 mph (238 km/h)

The excitement that can surround the announcement of a lost make's return to production often colors opinions of what its bikes will be like before they are even launched. Accordingly, the world's motorcycle press had high hopes for Morini's Corsaro and 9½ models. In this case, reality definitely failed to match expectation: when the first Corsaros hit the streets in June 2005 they were criticized for having poor ground clearance, snatchy throttle response and stiff gearboxes—and some wouldn't even start.

But, rather than explain away the faults as pre-production niggles, Morini went right back to the drawing board, returning six months later to relaunch a far better-finished, smoother, and generally more refined machine that is now a genuine alternative to a Ducati Monster or Triumph Speed Triple. This achievement is all the more impressive because the Corsaro's v-twin engine is a brand-new unit built by the bike manufacturer's sister firm, Morini Franco Motori, and designed by Franco Lambertini, who developed the legendary Moto Morini 3½ of the 1970s.

Tuned to produce lots of torque and to run smoothly at both high and low revs, the engine makes the Corsaro (Italian for "pirate") a versatile machine that can be trickled through traffic or wound up to more than 140 mph (225 km/h) on the open road. A Ducati-inspired trellis frame makes for fine handling, although Morini needs to work on slimming its pirate down a bit, as it weighs in at a swashbuckling 46 lb (21 kg) more than Ducati's more powerful Monster S4Rs.

Once a few hundred Corsaros are in circulation, expect this to develop into a well-finished, well-executed machine in the best naked tradition. The detuned and less brutal 9½ version should be even more pleasant as an everyday street bike, too.

Although few people could fault its looks, the original Brutale was something of a disappointment in the performance stakes, its four-cylinder, 750-cc engine providing neither the low-down grunt of a v-twin nor the top-end thrill of a larger-capacity triple or four.

That issue was addressed with the introduction of the 910S, which took the engine displacement to almost a liter and increased power to more than 97 kW (130 bhp), making the Brutale as mean as its name suggests it should be.

The new 910R adds to the package by improving the overall specification of the machine through the use of a competition exhaust system, race-quality Brembo Monoblock radially mounted brake calipers, larger, lighter brake discs, and forged aluminum wheel rims, also sourced from Brembo.

A strapping set of Marzocchi multiadjustable forks has been used to support the front end, while the rear suspension unit is the same as that fitted to MV's F4 1000 supersports machine.

MV claims that the Brutale 910R's engine is hand-finished, with extra polishing to the intake and exhaust ports to ensure a smoother gas flow, although a greater power boost is provided by the simple expedient of adding a more radical electronic chip to the engine-management system. Now the brute punches out 108 kW (145 bhp) and will sprint from 0 to 60 mph (97 km/h) in around three seconds, on its way to a maximum speed of 155 mph (249 km/h).

MV AGUSTA BRUTALE 910R

Engine
909 cc, double-overhead-camshaft, four-cylinder, four-stroke
Power
101 kW (136 bhp) @ 12,000 rpm
Torque
96 Nm (71 ft lb) @ 7900 rpm
Gearbox
Six-speed
Final drive
Chain
Weight
408 lb (185 kg)
Top speed
155 mph (249 km/h)

MZ SFX

As this book goes to press, MZ's brutal-looking SFX naked is still at the concept stage, but we're willing to gamble that by now it is ready to be included in the production lineup.

Although the MZ make was once unjustifiably derided when its output consisted solely of two-stroke, single-cylinder workhorses, the reborn brand now offers a genuine alternative to the mainstream products of Japan and Europe.

Based on the SF streetfighter, the SFX features the same parallel-twin engine and mainframe arrangement, but the overall styling is more extreme, with the rear frame tubes left exposed below the seat and the SF's bikini fairing junked in favor of a deep-set headlamp.

The twin upswept exhausts look the same as those fitted to the SF, but they also have been given a visual lift with a coating of matt-black paint.

"Low," "lean," and "mean" must have been the three key words in the brief handed to award-winning designer Jens von Brauck when he was asked to create the SFX, and he has certainly kept to them—although the "1050 cc" emblem on the side might just be wishful thinking: if the bike does make production, it is likely to be fitted with the same 998-cc, 87-kW (117 bhp) engine as both the SF and its sports-touring stablemate the S.

One feature they must retain, however, is their metallic-brown-and-black paint job: it sounds strange but it really works.

Engine
998 cc, liquid-cooled, double-overhead-camshaft, parallel-twin, four-stroke
Power
87 kW (117 bhp) @ 9000 rpm
Torque
95 Nm (70 ft lb) @ 7000 rpm
Gearbox
Six-speed
Final drive
Chain
Weight
441 lb (200 kg)
Top speed
135 mph (217 km/h)

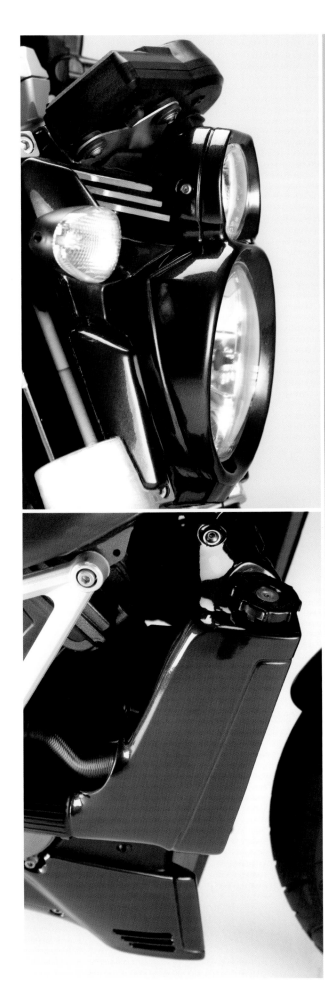

Suzuki's big-bore Bandit has been around for more than ten years, having been one of the first nakeds to appear on the market with a detuned sports bike engine and traditional styling at an affordable price. When first launched it was considered to be the ultimate hooligan machine and, thanks to its hugely powerful and torquey engine, it became a favorite of stunt-bike riders around the world for its wheelie-pulling ability.

The bulletproof mechanicals of the Bandit have ensured that the model has retained a loyal following, so it is no surprise to see that an upgraded version is keeping the model alive and well as part of Suzuki's latest lineup. The new model has been given a cosmetic makeover that endows it with a smoother, less aggressive appearance than that of its forebears.

Height-adjustable seats have been added to make the big Bandit more appealing to shorter riders, and there is a new swing arm and suspension setup at the rear for sweeter handling. The traditional analog clocks have been replaced by a digital LCD instrument panel and, for buyers of the SA version, which comes with a wind-tunnel tested fairing, the Bandit even gets ABS.

SUZUKI BANDIT GSF1200/ GSF1200SA

Engine
1157 cc, air-cooled, double-overhead-camshaft, four-cylinder, four-stroke
Power
78 kW (105 bhp) @ 8900 rpm (est.)
Torque
102 Nm (75 ft lb) @ 6000 rpm (est.)
Gearbox
Five-speed
Final drive
Chain
Weight
467 lb (212 kg); SA 474 lb (215 kg)
Top speed
145 mph (233 km/h); SA 150 mph (241 km/h)

SUZUKI GSR600

Although labeled a "hyper naked" by Suzuki, the new GSR600 is in reality no more "hyper" than Yamaha's FZ6 or even Honda's rather conservative Honda Hornet 600. The Suzuki's engine is lifted straight from the GSX-R600 supersports bike and slightly detuned before being slotted into a less radical chassis offering a comfortable, upright riding position.

The engine's power reduction—it produces about 11 kW (15 bhp) less than the sports bike—makes for a more tractable ride and ensures the GSR is practical as a town machine, although the 12,000-rpm red line means it can be made to scream delightfully on winding back roads.

A strong element of the bike's angular and futuristic styling is the twin spars of the aluminum frame, while the exhaust system terminates in a neat twin-muffler assembly tucked beneath the tail.

The fact that the GSR600 is intended as a first big bike for new riders is given away by a slight "budget" appearance and the use of merely adequate suspension and braking components. Even so, the engine and chassis should provide an excellent basis for aftermarket upgrades that could help to make a good machine into an excellent one.

Engine
599 cc, liquid-cooled, double-overhead-camshaft, four-cylinder, four-stroke
Power
72 kW (97 bhp) @ 12,000 rpm
Torque
60 Nm (44 ft lb) @ 10,000 rpm (est.)
Gearbox
Six-speed
Final drive
Chain
Weight
403 lb (183 kg)
Top speed
140 mph (225 km/h)

Yamaha's Fazer bikes have long been popular for providing practical, versatile transport with conventional yet eye-catching looks at a reasonable price. But, with the new FZ1 (naked) and FZ1 Fazer (bikini-faired), the firm is joining the ranks of manufacturers offering the power of a supersports bike combined with the comfort and practicality of an upright riding position.

The new Fazer's appearance is a bit more businesslike, too: check out the stubby, side-mounted exhaust pipe, the muscular line of the fuel tank, and the aggressive headlamp styling, all of which lend the unfaired version in particular a really mean presence.

But these bikes are not "all show and no go," as they are fitted with the ultrapowerful engine originally designed for Yamaha's king sports bike, the R1, which produces a massive 112 kW (150 bhp) at the crankshaft—sufficient to endow the Fazer with a top speed of 170 mph (274 km/h).

But although they undoubtedly have the outright power, the new Yamahas do lose out to their v-twin and three-cylinder naked competitors in one area: low-down thrust. One of the great appeals of a large-capacity street bike is usually its ability to pull hard and cleanly from low revs, making it as good at commuting as back-lane touring. With the FZ1 and Fazer, however, the rider is required to make use of the gearbox as if aboard a pure sports bike because the engine must be kept at the higher end of the rev range in order to keep it singing.

On highways and major roads this will not be a problem, and as a long-distance tourer the Fazer will undoubtedly prove to be a comfortable and capable mount, not least because of its large, split dual seat and the side cowlings and detachable side cases that are offered as optional extras.

Yet, while some will find town riding a chore, there will be plenty of riders who are willing to compromise for the bike's scorching main-road performance and, of course, those evil looks.

YAMAHA FZ1/ FZ1 FAZER

Engine
998 cc, liquid-cooled, double-overhead camshaft, four-cylinder, sixteen-valve, four-stroke
Power
110 kW (150 bhp) @ 11,000 rpm
Torque
106 Nm (78 ft lb) @ 8000 rpm
Gearbox
Six-speed
Final drive
Chain
Weight
FZ1 428 lb (194 kg); FZ1 Fazer 439 lb (199 kg)
Top speed
170 mph (274 km/h) (est.)

YAMAHA FZ6 ABS

Yamaha's middleweight FZ6 represents the ideal first "proper" motorcycle for a newly qualified rider: it is easy to handle and forgiving, but with more than sufficient power to provide a taste of superbike thrills.

It was probably this wish to appeal to novices that prompted Yamaha to fit the popular FZ6 with an optional antilock braking system: a good idea, as sudden panic braking is a common cause of accidents among fledgling riders, especially when performed on loose or slippery surfaces.

Yamaha's ABS is designed to keep the FZ6 looking good for longer, although it must be said that, even though the design was revamped in 2005, the baby FZ looks decidedly conservative next to its new one-liter brother.

There seems little doubt that a new FZ6 is already waiting in the wings and, as likely as not, that one will be based on the fabulous 2006 R6 supersports bike. Despite its comparatively staid looks, however, the current model remains an impressive machine, with its state-of-the-art two-part chassis, designed to make exploiting the bike's sprightly 73-kW (98 bhp) engine a pure joy.

As with the one-liter FZ, the 600-cc version is available in naked and half-faired variants.

Engine
600 cc, double-overhead-camshaft, four-cylinder, four-stroke
Power
73 kW (98 bhp) @ 12,000 rpm
Torque
63 Nm (46 ft lb) @ 10,000 rpm
Gearbox
Six-speed
Final drive
Chain
Weight
412 lb (187 kg)
Top speed
140 mph (225 km/h)

It is fair to say that the Ducati Multistrada started the trend for versatile street bikes that display trail styling but are not really intended to go off road. The MT-03 is Yamaha's take on the theme, a neat-looking machine that combines the grunty 660-cc engine from the XT trail bike with a sharp-handling road-bike frame and a commanding upright riding position.

This is a machine for the rider who doesn't care about traveling at sustained three-figure speeds or knocking a fraction of a second off the sprint from 0 to 60 mph (97 km/h). He or she (the MT0-3 is an excellent machine for women) simply wants a motorcycle that will get them from A to B through city traffic, but is also enough fun to make them want to ride it during weekends.

With its quick steering, tight turning circle and torquey "thumper" engine, the bike certainly makes the grade as a commuter, and its light weight, sharp handling and comfortable riding position also make it a winner on small roads. Yamaha has "tuned" the MT-03's exhaust note, too, for what it describes as "added grin factor" and the bike looks cool, too, especially with that horizontal, side-mounted single shock absorber.

A small range of official Yamaha extras is also available to personalize the MT-03, ranging from a practical paddock stand to a carbon-look rear seat cowl, wraparound handguards and a mini flyscreen. This is, however, exactly the type of motorcycle for which the aftermarket accessory producers love to create bolt-ons, so expect to see some radically modified MT-03s on the streets soon.

YAMAHA MT-03

Engine
660 cc, liquid-cooled, single-cylinder, four-valve, four-stroke
Power
33 kW (44 bhp) @ 6000 rpm
Torque
56 Nm (41 ft lb) @ 5250 rpm
Gearbox
Five-speed
Final drive
Chain
Weight
386 lb (175 kg)
Top speed
100 mph (161 km/h)

YAMAHA MT-0S

The MT-0S concept bike unveiled at the 2005 Paris show was everything many people had hoped Yamaha's MT-01 "torque sports" production machine would be, but wasn't—sadly, the MT-01 is far less radical in terms of both looks and performance than the buying public had anticipated.

At present the MT-0S remains very much a concept, but there's no doubt that if Yamaha offered it for sale in its current configuration it would sell like there's no tomorrow. Its fabulous looks might be expected to emerge from the workshops of a niche custom builder rather than a giant Japanese corporation, and the concept machine bristles with futuristic touches that combine with hot-rod looks to result in what might be called a "retro-futuristic" motorcycle.

A predictably massive v-twin engine (probably the 1670-cc unit from the MT-01) forms part of the structure of a minimalist frame, in which the rear shock absorber is almost hidden from view to give the impression that the back end—which does not benefit from a pillion seat—is almost floating on air. The swing arm is hewn from a chunk of billet aluminum and the final-drive sprocket is unconventionally mounted on its outside.

Up front, a headlamp and a driving lamp appear to be LED-powered, the speedometer and rev counter are combined into a single, round unit and a provocative red push-button marked "start" (just like those found in some high-performance cars) is mounted on top of the fuel tank, along with the lighting switch and various other controls.

The brakes are state-of-the-art radial calipers squeezing massive "breaking wave" discs, and to emphasize its raw and powerful nature the beast is fitted with giant air intakes and eye-catching triangulated high-level exhaust pipes.

It is highly unlikely that the MT-0S will ever make it to production form looking as brilliant as this and promising such torque-laden performance, but concept bikes are there to make us dream.

Specifications not available

Launched in 1985, the V-Max quickly became a motorcycling legend to rival the Triumph Bonneville or the Vincent Black Shadow. While it wasn't the outright fastest or best-handling motorcycle then available, it was certainly the most powerful and it had an awesome presence.

Strictly speaking a cruiser bike, the V-Max was the first of the breed to offer decent handling and truly startling straight-line performance, courtesy of its 1200-cc, v-four engine, which in "full power" form could punch out up to 104 kW (140 bhp).

Even though its technology has been overtaken many times during the past twenty-one years, the V-Max retains a loyal following, but sales in Europe have long been threatened by forthcoming new emission rules. This, along with the demands of V-Max fans for an all-new version, led Yamaha to unveil plans for the next-generation V-Max at the Tokyo show in the winter of 2005. The heritage of the proposed new model will be instantly recognizable from features such as the stepped seat, side-mounted air trumpets, minimal fuel tank, and stubby quad exhausts, but the frame and mechanics will be new from the ground up.

For a start, the engine is expected to displace around 1800 cc and be capable of producing a staggering 134 kW (180 bhp); instruments will be split between a handlebar-mounted display and a secondary unit on top of the fuel tank; massive disc brakes with radial calipers will slow the hefty beast down; and, to keep weight to a minimum, the frame will be made from cast aluminum.

It seems unlikely that Yamaha would tease V-Max fans with a prototype if it had no intention of producing the real thing, but it will probably be well into 2007 before the first production models appear on the road. The only bad news is that the machine's existence could prevent the equally radical twin-cylinder MT-05 ever being built.

YAMAHA V-MAX

Specifications not available

RETRO

DUCATI SPORT 1000

Engine
992 cc, fuel-injected, single-overhead-camshaft, l-twin, two-valve (Desmodromically operated), four-stroke
Power
63 kW (84 bhp) @ 8000 rpm
Torque
85 Nm (63 ft lb) @ 6000 rpm
Gearbox
Six-speed
Final drive
Chain
Weight
425 lb (193 kg)
Top speed
130 mph (209 km/h)

Back in 1973, Ducati came out with an eye-catching café racer called the 750 Sport that was immediately recognizable, with its distinctive, bright-yellow paint job and solo seat. Like all Ducatis, it handled better than the products of any other manufacturer, but its heavy controls and uncompromising riding position called for a special rider to master it—and that, of course, was part of its appeal. It was what nowadays might be called a "real motorcycle."

The new Sport 1000 evokes memories of those prized machines, with its stacked exhaust system, café-racer styling, and neat period touches, such as handlebar-end-mounted rearview mirrors, a smooth, chromed headlamp, and a deliciously retro racing stripe that segments the fuel tank and tailpiece. And look at those wheels: not only are the alloy rims laced with traditional spokes, but even the tires have been specially made to replicate a tread pattern from three decades ago.

Underneath its 1970s costume, though, this bike is right up to date, with upside-down Marzocchi forks, side-mounted, single rear shock absorber, twin 12.6-in. (320 mm) disc brakes matched to Brembo racing calipers and, of course, Ducati's 1000-cc "DS" twin-plug engine.

Fed by fuel injection, it is smooth and predictable at all speeds from walking pace to flat out, and there's even an electronically controlled stepper motor to make minute adjustments to the idling speed according to atmospheric variations. This last feature would surely have been welcomed by owners of the highly strung Ducati sports bikes of the 1970s.

Ducati really has captured the spirit of the age with this bike (particularly with the burnt-orange version, although black and red color schemes are also on offer). To turn it into a time machine, just add a rider in period leathers, goggles and skid lid, and find a good stretch of winding country road.

Anyone who thought Vincent had gone out of business in 1956 would be right, but this brilliant replica is as close as you're ever likely to get to owning a brand-new version of the real thing and, what's more, it's better.

Frenchman Patrick Godet is an internationally renowned Vincent restorer and racer who is building his own versions of the legendary Black Shadow high-performance model from the ground up, using entirely new manufactured components.

At the bike's heart is Godet's hand-assembled version of the glorious, 1000-cc, 47-degree v-twin powerplant that once made Vincents the world's fastest production motorcycles. His Black Shadow-specification engines are brought up to date with the use of electric starters and are built to minute tolerances to ensure oil tightness and modern-day reliability. Then they are fitted into the ultimate chassis for any Vincent engine: a perfect copy of the handbuilt, chrome-molybdenum frames originally made for the make by Swiss-born Fritz Egli, the 1960s hill-climb champion and king of the café racers.

Finishing touches include a handbuilt, siamesed exhaust system, rear-set footrests, spoked alloy rims and a huge twin-leading-shoe Fontana brake. The result is a fine-handling, lightweight superbike that, although based on a design more than half a century old, offers exceptional "real world" performance and rideability.

This example, one of a batch created by Godet for Dunhill, is finished in the luxury gentleman's outfitter's signature chocolate-brown paintwork and has a saddle hand-stitched by custom leather craftsman Bill Amberg.

GODET/EGLI VINCENT BLACK SHADOW

Engine
998 cc, v-twin, four-stroke
Power
Not available
Torque
Not available
Gearbox
Four-speed
Final drive
Chain
Weight
379 lb (172 kg)
Top speed
110 mph (177 km/h) (est.)

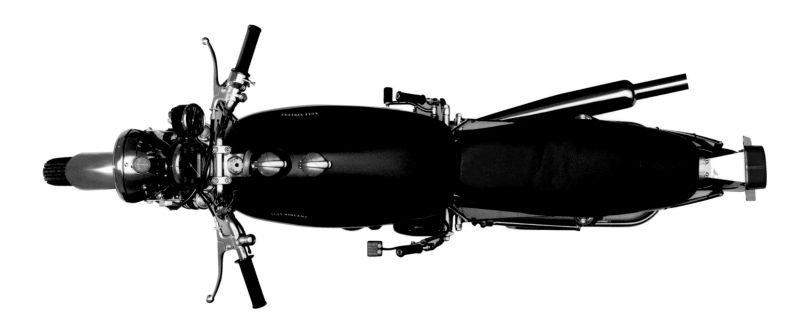

HARLEY-DAVIDSON FXD1 SUPER GLIDE ANNIVERSARY

Engine
1449 cc, air-cooled, 45-degree v-twin, four-stroke
Power
45 kW (60 bhp) (est.) @ 4800 rpm
Torque
106 Nm (78 ft lb) @ 4000 rpm
Gearbox
Six-speed
Final drive
Belt
Weight
639 lb (290 kg)
Top speed
110 mph (177 km/h) (est.)

While every air-cooled Harley-Davidson could be said to be "retro," the new thirty-fifth anniversary Super Glide is more retro than most, because it looks uncannily like the original machine it pays tribute to, right down to the distinctive red, white, and blue paint scheme.

The FX Super Glide of 1971 was born out of the 1960s chopper culture and was designed by Willie G. Davidson —who is still heavily involved in the design of modern Harleys—with the aim of creating a "drag bike" look by using a large rear tire and a big engine complemented by a minimalist front fork and wheel assembly.

This commemorative version achieves the look of the old but has a bit more "go," thanks to the use of the modern-day, 1449-cc, twin-cam engine with fuel injection and a six-speed gearbox. It stops better, too, because the original's fear-inducing drum brake has been replaced by a disc setup—although there is only one, when two would surely be more appropriate on a machine of this size and weight.

That engine, by the way, is also rubber-mounted, making the Anniversary far more pleasant to ride than the bike it emulates. But aside from all the engineering improvements, this bike is every bit as characterful as the 1970s model: it has the same small headlamp, the leather trim running down the centerline of the fuel tank, and the gently raised handlebars for the perfect laid-back, cruising look.

It just begs to be loaded up with a pair of leather panniers and a camping kit (or perhaps a guide to fine hotels) and ridden off into the California sunrise.

The Royal Enfield Bullet holds the record for the motorcycle in longest continuous production, having remained almost unchanged since its debut in 1949. Originally built in Redditch, England, it was licensed for manufacture to an Indian company in 1955 and has been made there ever since, despite the closure of the British firm in 1970.

Ironically, the Bullet is now more popular in Britain than anywhere else outside India, and is brought back to its roots by the UK importer Watsonian Squire. However, the model recently faced imminent demise as it seemed unlikely that its ancient engine would meet strict new EU regulations on emissions, due to be implemented in 2006.

The range has recently been added to, with the Electra Sportsman, a new, café-racer-style machine. Powered by the new lean-burn engine introduced by Royal Enfield in 2005 to meet strict new EU emissions limits, the Sportsman has an extra-large carburetor, a "free flow" exhaust system and a sportier air intake to boost power to an unremarkable 22 kW (30 bhp).

A single seat, dropped handlebars, rear-set footrests and a retro paint job give the bike a look similar to the make's Continental GT model of the mid-1960s, but there's no need to worry: it should be a lot more reliable than the original.

This bike is the perfect antidote to road-burning, huge-horsepower, multicylinder superbikes, being a delight for respectably brisk but law-abiding back-road riding. It's cheap to run, too, returning up to 26.5 kmpl (62.3 mpg) and there's even an electric starter for those who no longer want to pretend they have legs of steel.

ROYAL ENFIELD BULLET ELECTRA X

Engine
499 cc, air-cooled, single-cylinder, two-valve, four-stroke
Power
22 kW (30 bhp) @ 5500 rpm
Torque
47 Nm (35 ft lb) @ 3500 rpm
Gearbox
Five-speed
Final drive
Chain
Weight
353 lb (160 kg)
Top speed
80 mph (129 km/h)

TRIUMPH SCRAMBLER

If the late Steve McQueen is your hero and nostalgia is your bag, you'll be quickly sold on this latest take on the modern-day Bonneville. Triumph's "street scrambler" models of the 1960s were built mainly for the US market and had the sort of looks favored by the bike-mad star, who rode a Triumph in the cult film *The Great Escape*, famous for its fence-jumping scene.

This twenty-first-century street scrambler uses the Bonneville frame and powertrain married to a handsome set of high-level exhausts, wide, trail-style handlebars and chunky, dual-purpose tires. The retro styling is completed with rubber fork gaiters, a 19-in. (48.3 cm) front wheel, and a choice of classic 1960s two-tone paint jobs. The bike really looks the part and it sounds good, too.

But the Scrambler isn't just about keeping up off-road appearances, for it offers some trail capability. The high exhausts mean nothing much sticks out or hangs down to get caught on obstacles (an engine bash plate would be useful, though) and the torquey, low-revving engine delivers the right sort of power for gentle green-laning.

While nowhere near as light as a 'real' trail bike, this machine is well-balanced enough not to become hard to handle on the rough, and the off-road-oriented, upright riding position and wide handlebars also make it a very practical and maneuverable machine for city use.

No doubt the Scrambler will be embraced by "overland" riders seeking a taste of what globetrotting by motorcycle in the 1960s was like. It would be a good choice, with its modest off-road leanings and, of course, the mechanical reliability that those old Triumphs never really had.

Engine
865 cc, air-cooled, double-overhead-camshaft, parallel-twin, four-stroke
Power
40 kW (54 bhp) @ 7400 rpm
Torque
69 Nm (51 ft lb) @ 3700 rpm
Gearbox
Five-speed
Final drive
Chain
Weight
452 lb (205 kg)
Top speed
105 mph (169 km/h)

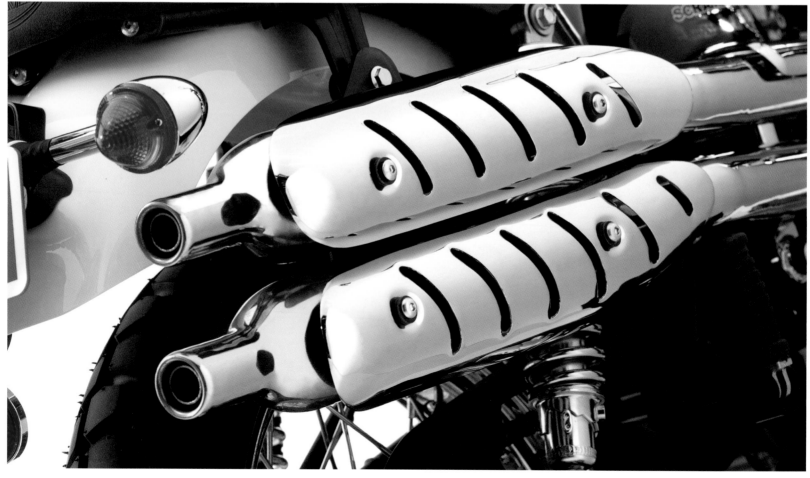

SCOOTERS
AND
MAXI SCOOTERS

Aprilia's Scarabeo 500 breaks the maxi-scooter mold by combining a large, single-cylinder engine with full-sized wheels to provide a commuter machine that is far more nimble and stable than its small-wheeled rivals.

But while the big Scarabeo is nippy in traffic, thanks to its quick steering and slim dimensions, it's powerful enough to take a rider and passenger away for a weekend jaunt fully laden with luggage, making light work of highways as though it were a full-fledged motorcycle.

The usual penalty for the extra stability provided by large wheels is that they encroach on luggage space, but Aprilia's engineers have managed to design the Scarabeo so that it has the most capacious storage compartment of any scooter of its type. Lift the seat and there's room for a full-face crash helmet or large briefcase, plus bits and pieces such as a mobile telephone, sunglasses, gloves, and waterproofs.

Add to this the optional quick-fit box that can be mounted on the parcel rack and the lockable storage area integrated into the leg shields, and you have a superpractical machine that is also fast and stylish.

Mindful that many Scarabeo buyers will be motorists recently converted to two wheels, the manufacturers have fitted the bike with a sophisticated linked braking system to reduce the risk of novices locking up a wheel in an emergency stop—the left-hand (rear) brake lever also activates one of the two front disc brakes.

A generous, 13.5-liter (3.6 US gallons) fuel tank ensures that the most can be made of the Scarabeo's long legs, too—with a potential fuel economy figure of around 18 kmpl (42 mpg), the bike has a range of up to 150 miles (241 km) between refills, so it really is a practical proposition for touring.

APRILIA SCARABEO 500

Engine
460 cc, fuel-injected, single-cylinder, four-valve, four-stroke
Power
29 kW (39 bhp) @ 7500 rpm
Torque
43 Nm (32 ft lb) @ 5500 rpm
Gearbox
Automatic
Final drive
Direct
Weight
417 lb (189 kg)
Top speed
85 mph (137 km/h)

GILERA RUNNER 198

Engine
50 cc, single-cylinder, two-stroke; or 125 cc, single-cylinder, four-stroke
Power
50 cc not available; 125 cc 11 kW (15 bhp) @ 9750 rpm
Torque
50 cc not available; 125 cc 12 Nm (9 ft lb) @ 8000 rpm
Gearbox
Single-speed, automatic
Final drive
Direct
Weight
50 cc 234 lb (106 kg); 125 cc 298 lb (135 kg)
Top speed
50 cc 30 mph (48 km/h); 125 cc 62 mph (100 km/h)

The Gilera Runner has become almost as much an icon of youth on two wheels as Vespa and Lambretta scooters were during the 1960s. It has dominated the "sports scooter" sector for almost a decade but, faced with stiff competition from the ever-cooler-looking machines being turned out by the opposition, Gilera has now given the Runner a major overhaul.

Designed as a scooter with the "soul" of a motorcycle, the Runner has bodywork and a seating position that are more akin to those of a bike. In addition, the machine's ergonomics have been fine-tuned to improve rider control and enhance handling, which, for a scooter, is unusually reassuring, thanks to a low center of gravity and an exceptionally rigid frame.

The old 12-in. (30 cm) wheels, often a source of twitchy handling, have been replaced with a 14-in. (35.6 cm) front and a 13-in. (33 cm) rear, both equipped with fat, sporty tires.

The Runner is available with a choice of 50-cc two-stroke engines—one carburetor-fed, the other fuel-injected—or a four-stroke 125-cc unit that provides brisk acceleration and a top speed in excess of 60 mph (97 km/h).

The Chinese-built Hero Nipster didn't qualify for a place in this book because of its innovative engineering, stunning looks, or impressive performance—it boasts none of the above.

What it does do, however, is present the chance to take to two wheels on a brand-new machine at the lowest possible price. In the UK, the Nipster retails for less than $1800 ready to go. It offers a top speed of a meager 28 mph (45 km/h), its build quality is some way from equalling that of its Japanese and Italian rivals, and it has no fancy features such as a linked braking system or an adjustable windshield.

For a crosstown commute, however, it is pretty difficult to beat: with miserly fuel consumption of 43 kmpl (101 mpg) or more, minuscule dimensions that make it easy to maneuver and park, and practical, anti-scratch bodywork, it's the perfect starter machine. Hero also produces the similarly austere 125-cc Quickster and the sporty-looking Slickster, as well as two budget motorcycles, the Magellan trail bike and the Pluto cruiser (pp. 106–107).

HERO NIPSTER

Engine
49 cc, air-cooled, single-cylinder, four-stroke
Power
1 kW (2 bhp) @ 6000 rpm
Torque
4 Nm (3 ft lb) @ 3500 rpm
Gearbox
Automatic
Final drive
Direct
Weight
353 lb (160 kg)
Top speed
28 mph (45 km/h)

HONDA PS125i

Commuter scooters have become so popular nowadays that the major manufacturers seem to be spending almost as much time creating new ones as they devote to developing their more sophisticated machines. Honda continues to enjoy worldwide success with its large-wheeled, four-speed Innova, the modern-day version of its legendary Cub, which is still available in some countries forty years after its introduction.

However, many new riders are daunted by bikes with a foot-change gearbox, and it's for them that the PS125i is intended. This smart new town scooter uses Honda's latest low-emission, fuel-injected, four-stroke engine, which offers exceptional fuel economy—in excess of 36 kmpl (85 mpg)—while providing the low-down pulling power that novices need for a wobble-free takeoff when getting accustomed to riding a motorized two-wheeler.

Designed to look friendly and not at all forbidding, the PS125i has plenty of smooth, curving contours. The large seat almost dominates the machine, being long and wide and extending toward the footboards for maximum comfort. It conceals a usefully large storage compartment big enough for a full-face crash helmet, and more carrying capacity is provided by the rear parcel rack, which is a standard fitting.

Honda has given the PS125i extra-wide footboards to keep road dirt off its chic riders' expensive footwear, and there is also a leg-shield-mounted carrying hook from which to suspend a designer briefcase.

Engine
125 cc, liquid-cooled, single-cylinder, four-stroke
Power
10 kW (13 bhp) @ 9000 rpm
Torque
12 Nm (9 ft lb) @ 7000 rpm
Gearbox
Automatic
Final drive
Direct
Weight
298 lb (135 kg)
Top speed
55 mph (88 km/h)

Honda's 600-cc Silver Wing is regarded as a benchmark in the maxi-scooter class, thanks to its legendary speed, smoothness, finish and reliability. Indeed, many owners who bought one to complement a "proper" motorcycle have found that the "Wing" not only is more convenient for commuting, but also makes a better all-rounder.

Like Suzuki with its latest Burgman, Honda has now decided to introduce a 400-cc variant of the Silver Wing for riders who don't necessarily need the larger machine's powerful cruising capability. The Silver Wing 400, however, retains exactly the same chassis and bodywork as the 600 and, unlike the 400 Burgman with its single-cylinder engine, it is powered by the refined twin-cylinder configuration of its bigger brother.

Short to medium-range commuting is what Honda's new 400 is designed for, and to that end it is brimming with practical features. The fairing incorporates one-touch, weather-sealed glove boxes; the underseat storage capacity takes what Honda describes as a "monstrous" load of shopping. Optional extras abound: a cargo net to enable luggage to be carried on the pillion seat; a 45-liter (1.6 cu. ft) top box with a removable inner bag; electrically heated handlebar grips; leg deflectors; and even a taller windshield.

A 16-liter (4.2 US gallons) fuel tank allows a respectable 150-miles (241 km) range and, to make the Silver Wing as easy to use as possible, Honda has given it linked brakes and a special center stand to facilitate parking what is, despite its baby-brother status, still quite a hefty machine.

HONDA SILVER WING

Engine
398 cc, liquid-cooled, double-overhead-camshaft, twin-cylinder, eight-valve, four-stroke
Power
27 kW (36 bhp) @ 8000 rpm
Torque
37 Nm (27 ft lb) @ 6500 rpm
Gearbox
Automatic
Final drive
Shaft
Weight
503 lb (228 kg)
Top speed
85 mph (137 km/h)

PIAGGIO X8 PREMIUM

With its 250-cc engine, Piaggio's X8 only just qualifies for the maxi-scooter class in terms of power and performance, but for practicality, ease of use, and efficiency it is probably one of the best maxis on the market.

The single-cylinder engine has enough get up and go to carry two people along at more than respectable speeds, and it is up to tackling the occasional highway blast and long-distance jaunt. Yet the overall size of the X8, compared with half-liter scooters, makes it much more manageable in the urban situations where it is most likely to find use.

An extra-large underseat storage area swallows work bags and shopping, being accessed by raising either the seat or the neat flip-up "trunk lid" at the rear. There is enough space for two full-face crash helmets and other objects measuring up to about 30 in. (75 cm) in length, while the front shield contains a handy cubby hole fitted with a 12-volt plug for recharging a mobile telephone. Add the optional rear rack and 48-liter (1.7 cu. ft) top box, and this scooter is transformed into a two-wheeled storeroom offering over 100 liters (3.5 cu. ft) of capacity.

Considerably more economical on fuel than its 500-cc rivals, the X8 easily achieves 18 kmpl (42 mpg) around town, allowing over 150 miles (241 km) between fill-ups. In addition, its state-of-the-art fuel-injection system ensures low emissions and excellent cold starting.

Engine
244 cc, liquid-cooled, single-cylinder, four-valve, four-stroke
Power
16 kW (22 bhp) @ 8250 rpm
Torque
20 Nm (15 ft lb) @ 6500 rpm
Gearbox
Automatic
Final drive
Direct
Weight
392 lb (178 kg)
Top speed
75 mph (121 km/h)

Suzuki's 650-cc Burgman Executive is one of the most stylish, best-equipped and downright luxurious maxi scooters on the market. But what if you just want to get from A to B and don't need all the extras?

The answer is here in the shape of the new Burgman 400, which offers Burgman styling and comfort similar to that of its big brother, but costs considerably less and can be ridden by license holders not qualified to take to the road on a two-wheeler as powerful as the 650.

The 400's single-cylinder engine makes the bike somewhat less smooth and refined than the 650, with its twin cylinders, but it still offers brisk acceleration and a useful top speed of around 75 mph (121 km/h).

That large, comfortable-looking seat conceals a huge 53-liter (1.9 cu. ft) storage space that Suzuki has thoughtfully illuminated, and it also incorporates a rider's backrest that can be adjusted between five different positions for complete comfort.

The wide, weather-beating windshield is also multiadjustable and is provided with an aerodynamic antibuffeting vent to prevent the Burgman being blown off course when traveling at speed. A linked braking system whereby the left-hand lever operates the front and rear brakes simultaneously is also part of the package, although the 400 is not available with the excellent ABS system fitted to the 650 Executive.

SUZUKI BURGMAN 400

Engine
385 cc, liquid-cooled, single-cylinder, four-valve, four-stroke
Power
24 kW (32 bhp) @ 7500 rpm
Torque
32 Nm (24 ft lb) @ 6000 rpm
Gearbox
Automatic
Final drive
Direct
Weight
406 lb (184 kg)
Top speed
75 mph (121 km/h) (est.)

VESPA GTS 250 ie

The Piaggio Vespa—Italian for 'wasp'—has been around for almost sixty years, but the latest models arrive with more of a whisper than an insect-like buzz, thanks to their ultrarefined, four-stroke engines. Strict worldwide emission regulations have made manufacturers such as Piaggio work hard to produce quieter, greener machines, but not only have they managed to stick to the rules, they've also enhanced performance.

As a result, the GTS 250 is the fastest, most powerful Vespa ever. Inspired by the 1950s GS—the hot-rod scooter of its day—the new machine features bodywork that hints at the look of the old, but everywhere else it is entirely cutting-edge.

Electronic fuel injection (indicated by the Italian suffix "ie"), an electric starter and rather more than 15 kW (20 bhp) at the end of the twist grip are joys that the Mods of old would probably never have thought possible, but the GTS has them all.

Keeping faith with the old days, however, the daddy Vespa's look is set off by heavy chroming on the front mudguard and rack, as well as a neat driving lamp set into the front panel. And, for those who want to play up the Mod associations, an extensive chroming kit is an optional extra.

Other accessories include a large top box with a built-in pillion backrest, a custom-designed canvas bag complete with laptop carrier, a windshield, and a fleece-lined leg wrap.

Engine
244 cc, fuel-injected, single-cylinder, four-valve, four-stroke
Power
16 kW (22 bhp) @ 8500 rpm
Torque
20 Nm (15 ft lb) @ 6500 rpm
Gearbox
Single-speed, automatic
Final drive
Direct
Weight
333 lb (151 kg)
Top speed
75 mph (121 km/h)

Yamaha's T-Max 500 set a new standard for large-engined scooters when it was launched back in 2001 because it combined 100-mph (161 km/h) performance with sharp, taut handling, and a roadholding ability previously unheard of on a "twist-and-go" machine.

Much of the T-Max's success could be attributed to Yamaha's innovative use of larger-than-normal wheels (for a scooter)—a 14-in. (35.6 cm) front and a 16-in. (41 cm) rear—and to its rigid "diamond" frame. Many of the design features that made the bike such a success have now been scaled down to create two new models: the 125-cc and the 250-cc X-Max. With smaller fairings, shorter wheelbases, and less weight, these offer the same sporty feel as the half-liter machine, but are far more maneuverable in traffic and easier to squeeze into those ever more elusive parking spaces in cities.

Although the 125-cc X-Max is aimed at new riders and doesn't offer the 500's versatility in terms of being able to cruise on the highway as well as cut through traffic, the 250-cc version is an excellent compromise between the two. Usefully lighter in town, it's powerful enough for occasional distance work and offers great comfort and a capacious underseat carrying capacity.

YAMAHA X-MAX 125/250

Engine
124 cc/249 cc, liquid-cooled, single-cylinder, four-stroke
Power
125 10 kW (14 bhp) @ 8750 rpm; 250 24 kW (32 bhp) @ 7500 rpm
Torque
125 11 Nm (8 ft lb) @ 6500 rpm; 250 21 Nm (15 ft lb) @ 6250 rpm
Gearbox
Automatic
Final drive
Direct
Weight
125 337 lb (153 kg); 250 362 lb (164 kg)
Top speed
125 60 mph (97 km/h); 250 75 mph (121 km/h)

ODDBALLS

DERBI GPX1 XPERIMENT

At the time of writing, the GPX1 was still just an "Xperiment," but the theory behind it seems so sound that there is every chance that the bike will soon be in the showrooms. Designer José González set out to create an easy-to-handle, supermoto-style machine that would not intimidate new riders.

He has given it the butch, chunky looks of a full-size motorcycle, but it is powered by the simple, twist-and-go 50-cc engine and automatic transmission system used in the GP1 scooter. The nearest comparable machine currently on the market is Gilera's DNA scooter/motorcycle hybrid, but the GPX1 makes that look rather outdated.

This latest Derbi design is expected to be grouped in the company's Mulhacén family, which will comprise an entire range of road bikes with engine capacities of up to 650 cc.

It seems likely that, before long, twist-and-go machines with the look of the GPX1 but powered by engines of, say, 250 cc or even larger will start to be produced by the major manufacturers as an alternative to conventional scooters.

Specifications not available

DERBI RAMBLA

The Spanish manufacturer Derbi is gaining quite a reputation for making radical-looking bikes—check out the retro-cool Mulhacén featured in *The New Motorcycle Yearbook 1.*

Dreamed up by the same designer, this peculiar scooterlike machine is brimming with neat features, such as a backrest that folds down into a pillion seat, a frame that snakes around the outside of the bodywork to protect it in a spill, and a choice of wheel sizes: 12-in. (30 cm) ones for road use and 15-in. (38 cm) ones fitted with knobbly tires for off-road riding.

The front mudguard is also pretty nifty because it doubles up as a flat luggage platform. The Rambla, which will be available with a choice of 50-cc or 125-cc engine when it goes on sale in 2007, has already been dubbed the "SUV of scooters." Who knows, maybe this could be the start of a whole new trend.

Engine
50 cc, single-cylinder, two-stroke;125 cc, single-cylinder, four-stroke
Power
Not available
Torque
Not available
Gearbox
Automatic
Final drive
Direct
Weight
Not available
Top speed
50 cc 30 mph (48 km/h); 125 cc 55 mph (88 km/h)

ELECTRICMOTO BLADE T6

Engine
Electric brush-type motor
Power
19 kW (26 electrical hp)
Torque
Not available
Gearbox
Single-speed automatic
Final drive
Chain
Weight
165 lb (75 kg)
Top speed
40 mph (64 km/h)

To the antimotorcycle lobby, dirt bikes represent the ultimate in two-wheeled political uncorrectness. Dogmatic thinkers who loathe off-road motorcycles with a vengeance usually cite their noise as the first reason for banning them, before going on to blame them for everything from global warming to scaring the horses.

What, then, will they make of the ElectricMoto Blade, a dirt bike that promises to keep up with a gas-engined 250-cc motocrosser without creating any noise or pollution? It sounds too good to be true, but the Blade really is the ultimate in electric, high-performance off-roaders, combining light weight with a genuine rear-wheel power output of 13 kW (18 bhp). It weighs, with its battery, a meager 165 lb (75 kg) and comes equipped with high-quality components such as Ohlins motocross forks with 12 in. (30.5 cm) of suspension travel, an Ohlins rear shock and large hydraulic disc brakes.

The only thing the Blade lacks is the thrilling "blat" of a four-stroke motocrosser or the spine-tingling "zing" of a two-stroke. Imagine, if this is the future of off-road racing, how soulless it will be to watch an event where thirty machines are charging around berms, flying off jumps, and pulling monster wheelies—all in near silence.

Where the Blade really scores, however, is in its suitability as a recreational off-road bike for leisure use. Most restrictions on the use of motorcycles in forests, parks, and other country areas usually apply only to those powered by internal combustion engines, but no doubt the killjoys will adapt these rules once they learn how much fun bikes such as the Blade are.

The ENV, or Emissions Neutral Vehicle, is the world's first purpose-built motorcycle powered by a hydrogen fuel cell. It is the product of British firm Intelligent Energy, which has taken five years to create a practical application for a type of hydrogen-fuel-cell technology that Loughborough University spent fifteen years developing and which, incidentally, was discovered as a principle back in 1830.

Intelligent Energy, which calls itself an "energy solutions company," commissioned award-winning design house Seymourpowell (creator of the MZ Skorpion motorcycle and consultant to BMW Motorrad) to design the ENV around the core of a compact hydrogen fuel cell. This is of the Proton Exchange Membrane type (PEM), acting as a catalyst to produce water and electricity from a charge of hydrogen and oxygen. A three-minute fill-up of hydrogen is sufficient to power the ENV at speeds of up to 50 mph (80 km/h) for around four hours, with the bike emitting nothing more unpleasant than water vapor along the way.

Hydrogen is the world's most plentiful element, as well as being a clean, efficient fuel, and the ENV is as quiet as a conventional electric motorcycle in operation. The first batch is expected to go on sale in California in mid-2007 at a cost of $10,000 each, and Intelligent Energy is already perfecting a hydrogen creator that can make the element from crop fuels such as bioethanol.

The PEM cell is particularly suitable for a powered two-wheeler because of its size, weight and robustness—a test-bed version of the cell has clocked 16,000 hours without any sign of deterioration. It consists of a multilayered 'sandwich' of graphite plates and Membrane Electrode Assemblies (MEAs). The MEAs work as a catalyst in an electrochemical reaction to produce electricity from a combination of 99.9% pure hydrogen and oxygen from the atmosphere.

For sound environmental reasons, machines such as the ENV are clearly the way forward. The only likely stumbling block to their becoming the norm sooner rather than later is our reluctance to give up the sound, smell, feel, and familiarity of the gas-engined bikes we have come to love.

ENV (EMISSIONS NEUTRAL VEHICLE)

Engine
6-kW (8 bhp) brush motor with 1-kW (1 bhp) air-cooled hydrogen fuel cell
Power
2 kW (3 bhp)
Torque
Not available
Gearbox
Automatic, variable transmission
Final drive
Belt
Weight
176 lb (80 kg)
Top speed
50 mph (80 km/h)

Pull up at your local motorcycle club meet on this beast and you're sure to turn a few heads: this is the machine that proves without doubt that Harley-Davidsons can be blindingly fast.

Based on the already quick and powerful V-Rod road bike, the Destroyer is a limited-edition special built and designed by Harley's Custom Vehicle Operations (CVO) and is intended purely for competitive drag racing.

Most drag bikes are put together by their engineer riders and involve hundreds of hours of painstaking construction—after which they often blow up at the vital moment. The Destroyer, however, offers a reliable, factory-built solution for the lazy drag racer, so long as he or she has the $37,000-plus required to buy it (which is actually very reasonable considering how much money and effort it would take for a private individual to create something similar).

The Harley-Davidson factory-backed drag team has held the American Pro Stock championship title for two years in a row, running a similar bike to the Destroyer, which uses the same basic frame and swing arm as the V-Rod but with a wildly tuned engine that pumps out 123 kW (165 bhp).

It does its "screamin'" through an open exhaust system, and the lightning-fast gear changes required on the drag strip are performed through a set of handlebar-mounted buttons that activate an air shifter. An ignition cutout kills the engine for a fraction of a second between the gears, enabling the throttle to be kept wide open all the way through the gearbox.

To put the power on the ground the bike also has a lock-up clutch that can be engaged at maximum revs, and a massive, 7.9-in. (200 mm) wide slick rear tire, and to keep the whole thing from simply flipping over backward, a specially fabricated "wheelie bar" is bolted on the end.

In the hands of a drag-race star, the Destroyer will eat up 0.25 mile (400 m) in a mind-blowing nine seconds, and even with a mediocre pilot aboard it can easily crack the magic 11-second barrier that was once every dragger's goal.

Imagine having a road-legal version of this to teach all those boy racers a lesson at the traffic light GP.

HARLEY-DAVIDSON V-ROD 'SCREAMIN' EAGLE' DESTROYER

Engine
1300 cc, liquid-cooled, double-overhead-camshaft, v-twin, four-stroke
Power
123 kW (165 bhp) @ 9700 rpm
Torque
132 Nm (97 ft lb) @ 8000 rpm
Gearbox
Five-speed
Final drive
Chain
Weight
525 lb (238 kg)
Top speed
Not available

MTT Y2K JET BIKE

Dedicated followers of the world's fastest motorcycles will know that the MTT Y2K jet bike first appeared at Daytona Speed Week back in 2000, but it's included in the current *New Motorcycle Yearbook* because that initial experiment in engineering madness attracted so much attention that the machine has now gone into full production.

The Y2K is simply the fastest, most powerful road-going machine you can buy: it is propelled by a Rolls-Royce Allison 250 series gas turbine that runs on AvGas, or, in an emergency, plain old diesel. The Allison turbine is more commonly found in helicopters, but Y2K's Louisiana-based designer Ted McIntyre realized that the output shaft normally used to drive a chopper's blades could easily be adapted for motorcycle use.

Among the many benefits of a gas turbine are a total lack of vibration, massive power, excellent reliability, and, of course, that fabulous turbine whine. The drawbacks are airplane-like fuel consumption and the fact that turbines get extremely hot and prefer to run at constant speeds rather than being asked to keep changing revs, as they are on a road-going motorcycle. You'll also need to relearn how to ride, as there is a total lack of engine braking.

Just two gears are needed: one for pulling away and the other for projecting the machine into infinity, both being controlled by handlebar-mounted switches.

All the bodywork on the Y2K is made from carbon fiber specially made to resist the turbine's heat, while the bike's space-age credentials are reinforced with the addition of a comprehensive array of aviation-style electronics, including a rearview television screen that enables the rider to see what he has left behind in the turbine blast.

Fancy one? Then join the queue leading to Ted McIntyre's door at MTT (Marine Turbine Technologies)—with a check for $250,000.

Engine
Rolls-Royce Allison 250 gas turbine
Power
239 kW (320 bhp) @ 54,000 rpm
Torque
577 Nm (425 ft lb) @ 18,000 rpm
Gearbox
Two-speed with electronic shift
Final drive
Chain
Weight
500 lb (227 kg)
Top speed
Ostensibly 250 mph (402 km/h) but, in reality, until you daren't go any faster

French manufacturer Scorpa is best known for producing highly competitive and moderately priced trials motorcycles powered by Yamaha engines, but the bike that has really put the company's name on the map is the 4-Tricks.

Inspired by the "X-Generation's" fascination with motorcycle stunt competitions, the machine is an ultralight powered two-wheeler that is as much mountain bike as motorcycle. Tiny, supermaneuverable and robust, it is built specifically for what its name says.

The engine is a puny 70-cc Yamaha four-stroke, but because the machine is very light—some riders will be able to hoist it above their heads as it's not much heavier than a sack of potatoes—it doesn't need much power in order to deliver off-the-throttle wheelies and grapple its way up the steepest inclines.

Rather like the more sophisticated Yamaha Tricker and Tricker Pro, the 4-Tricks is one of those little motorbikes that look as though they are really for kids, but that no adventurous adult could resist having some fun on. It is equipped with double-piston Magura disc brakes at front and rear—for impressive "stoppies" and slides—and its 51-cm (20 in.) wheels are fitted with grippy trials-pattern tires.

The diminutive, single-cylinder engine is protected by an aluminum skid plate, which also makes it easier to slide the 4-Tricks over rocks and tussocks, and the bike is fitted with wide, pivoting footrests and a fully enclosed chain guard for safety. Fuel is carried in the frame tube.

SCORPA 4-TRICKS

Engine
70 cc, single-overhead-camshaft, single-cylinder, four-stroke
Power
6 kW (8 bhp)
Torque
Not available
Gearbox
Four-speed, automatic
Final drive
Chain
Weight
79 lb (36 kg)
Top speed
40 mph (64 km/h)

VECTRIX

Engine
Brushless-electric, direct-current, radial-air-gap motor
Power
20 kW (26 bhp equivalent) @ 3000 rpm
Torque
65 Nm (48 ft lb) from standstill
Gearbox
Automatic with slow-speed reverse
Final drive
Direct
Weight
437 lb (198 kg)
Top speed
62 mph (100 km/h)

Lots of vehicles claim to be the transport solutions of the future, but in the case of the Vectrix such words might actually be justified. This is the world's first genuine, high-performance, electrically powered maxi scooter—and it really works. One of the people behind its development, Carlo di Biaggio, is a former Ducati executive, so he knows the motorcycle industry inside out, and clearly believes machines such as the Vectrix to be the way forward.

Until now, most electric scooters have suffered from poor build quality, pathetic performance, feeble range and excess weight, but the Vectrix takes care of all those problems by offering a top speed of 62 mph (100 km/h), a 0–60 mph (0–97 km/h) time of just 6.8 seconds, and handling and finish in the league of the best Japanese gas-engined maxi scooters.

Neat touches include a multifunction throttle that, when backed off, induces effective engine braking and also puts a small amount of electrical charge (between 8 and 12%) back into the battery, which helps contribute to the machine's range of 68 miles (109 km). There is even a slow-speed reverse gear to assist parking.

Handling is excellent, thanks to the use of 14-in. (35.6 cm) front and 13-in. (33 cm) rear wheels, while high-tech equipment includes a Bluetooth diagnostic and communications system and an onboard computer that supplies information about battery status, electricity consumption and remaining range.

The Vectrix costs about the same to buy as a conventional, large-engined scooter, but is said to cost just a tenth of the price to run, while producing zero emissions. In addition, it accelerates 30% faster than a gas-engined, 250-cc automatic. This is because an electric motor makes its maximum torque at extremely low revs, which, in the case of the Vectrix, is an impressive 65 Nm (48 ft lb) from standstill. Its peak power output is also more than ten times that of most of its rivals.

On the practical side, it offers just as much underseat storage space as any of its conventional competitors and its battery can be fully recharged from a household electrical socket in just two hours. This means that the Vectrix could be used for quite long commutes without the rider having to worry whether or not it will have enough energy left to get him or her home again.

A brilliant machine.

VIALLI CARGO LPG

If you're environmentally friendly, are exceptionally parsimonious, need plenty of carrying capacity and don't mind being seen on a very unattractive scooter, the Vialli Cargo might be the answer to your two-wheeled prayers.

The average 50-cc, four-stroke bike will easily return 35.8 kmpl (84.2 mpg), but because the Vialli is powered by Liquid Petroleum Gas (LPG), which is less than half the price of gas (in the UK, at least), effectively it costs the same to run as a conventional moped that consumes half as much gas. LPG conversions have been popular in gas-guzzling cars since the 1980s— even Britain's Prime Minister is wafted around in one in an attempt to seem environmentally friendly and cash-conscious. The drawback with LPG at the moment is that the majority of filling stations don't sell it, although the number that do is said to be increasing.

That aside, LPG does have the benefit of producing around 50% lower carbon monoxide emissions than gas and 40% fewer hydrocarbons. But since a conventional 50-cc engine creates such a minuscule amount of greenhouse gases and costs so little to run anyway, the question must be asked: what's the point?

The Cargo is the most practical of a range of Chinese-built LPG machines distributed by Vialli. It doesn't look great, but it's cheap to buy, is ridiculously cheap to run, and has lots of carrying capacity. Just make sure you live close to an LPG source before you buy one. And, if you decide to go on a 30-mph (48 km/h) world tour, remember that LPG-powered vehicles are invariably banned from long tunnels.

Engine
49 cc, single-cylinder, four-stroke
Power
1 kW (2 bhp) @ 7000 rpm
Torque
Not available
Gearbox
Automatic
Final drive
Direct
Weight
172 lb (78 kg)
Top speed
30 mph (48 km/h)

KEY
DESIGNERS

LARRY NAGEL AND PAUL YANG
Dreamcraft Studios

Until the summer of 2004, the wider world hadn't heard much about Larry Nagel and Paul Yang—indeed, only two years earlier they hadn't even heard of each other. Now, however, they are firmly established among the elite of today's most innovative, imaginative, and talented designers of custom motorcycles.

But there is little chance that you'll ever see one of the wondrous creations that emerge from Nagel and Yang's Dreamcraft Studios cruise past you on the street. These are exclusive machines built in Ontario, California, for exclusive people and, as such, they have highly exclusive price tags, with an entry-level example costing a cool $100,000.

Like many success stories, international recognition for Dreamcraft came about almost by accident. In the summer of 2002, Nagel pinned a postcard to the bulletin board at the Art Center College of Design in Pasadena, California. It read quite simply: "Wanted: designer to help design a concept motorcycle. Call Larry, Dreamcraft Studios."

The advertisement caught the eye of Yang while he was visiting a friend at the college, which is responsible for producing half of all the world's automotive designers and where he himself had studied. A few days later he was showing his impressive portfolio to Nagel, who liked what he saw.

Nagel recalls: "I had spoken to other designers already, but one look at Paul's portfolio quite simply blew me away and I asked him there and then to help me create a one-shot concept bike. One of the reasons

I wanted to work with him was, strangely enough, because he had never designed a motorcycle before. To me, that meant he had no preconceptions and therefore no barriers to overcome—he could just create whatever was in his imagination."

At this point it should be noted that to be able to present his prospective colleague with a portfolio good enough to "blow him away" means that Yang must have quite a gift. Nagel's past solo projects have included the outrageous Vorian, a full-size version of a child's transformer toy that can "grow" into a 40-foot (12 m) monster that breathes fire through a pair of steel nostrils. He also hand-built the 300-mph (480 km/h) Pocket Rocket, the world's smallest and fastest hydrogen-powered vehicle, as well as numerous drag racers and alcohol-fuelled "funny cars."

The first fruit of the pair's collaboration was the DCS-001 Saga (featured in *The New Motorcycle Yearbook 1* and pictured on the front cover of the US edition), which was intended to be nothing more than a demonstration of the custom builder's art. However, its appearance at the Los Angeles Art Center Classic Car Show in July 2004 attracted the eye of a journalist from America's "bible of the rich," The Robb Report, who said that the machine was worthy of inclusion in the publication's annual Ultimate Gift Guide. In order to qualify, however, the machine had to be not just a one-shot experiment, but a motorcycle that was on sale with a retail price tag, so that it could be bought by a seeker of "the ultimate gift."

> **"One look at Paul's portfolio quite simply blew me away and I asked him there and then to help me create a one-shot concept bike."**
> Larry Nagel

The bike subsequently appeared in the guide—and was bought—and so it was that a Dreamcraft machine became the latest must-have for super-rich shoppers who appreciate the custom firm's philosophy that every project is as individual as its owner, so no two will ever be the same.

In the hands of lesser designers than Yang and lesser engineers than Nagel, the DCS-001 would never have had its genesis. As Nagel explains: "Previously I only really understood how to work alone and, at first, I didn't really think I would be able to operate as part of a team, particularly with such a young designer. Paul kept coming out with all sorts of wild ideas that I said simply wouldn't work, but in the end I just said dream up whatever you like and, if it's physically possible, I'll make it. After all, I did originally say that I wanted to create a motorcycle that would ignore every typical design idea, so it was never going to be easy."

Remarkably, the entire project was completed without the use of modern, computer-controlled tooling. The handlebars, for example, began life as a length of metal tubing 0.75 in. (19 mm) diameter that Nagel packed with sand before sealing at each end. He then attached the tube to a hand-made jig and heated it with a welding torch until the metal began to bend and droop in the right places. It took him just a few minutes, but the complex handlebar structure is perfectly symmetrical and appears to have been machine-made.

The 695-lb (315 kg) Saga took seven months to construct and, as explained in *The New Motorcycle*

Yearbook 1, it has no metal or plastic bodywork and uses a frame that both provides the structural backbone of the machine and gives it its overall form. Unsurprisingly, the machine attracted considerable interest and Dreamcraft's order book for 2005 was filled to capacity, with particular enthusiasm being shown by a new breed of motorcycle buyer: the super-rich tycoon.

Once the ultimate symbol of rebellion and non-conformity, a low-slung, raked-out, bad-ass chopper has become the latest desirable accessory for corporate millionaires, television celebrities, and sports stars who are willing to spend hundreds of thousands of dollars on a machine that they will seldom ride for more than a couple of minutes—and never in the wet.

"Motorcycles are fast becoming status symbols and the high-end machines such as we make are not being bought by motorcyclists but by people who want to own a one-of-a-kind artwork," says Nagel. "The fact is, anyone who is reasonably rich can own a Ferrari, but clients come to us because every bike we make is unique and their main criterion is to have something that no one else can ever buy."

The international acclaim achieved by the Saga, combined with the emergence of this new order of motorcyclists, has resulted in the latest Dreamcraft designs: the possibly even more outrageous Rapture featured in the Cruisers section of this book (a machine built at the behest of a fanatical and super-rich collector of rare cars and motorcycles) and the DCS-004 Synergy. Dreamcraft describes the second as its "glimpse into

Above
Dreamcraft's radical DCS-002 Rapture.

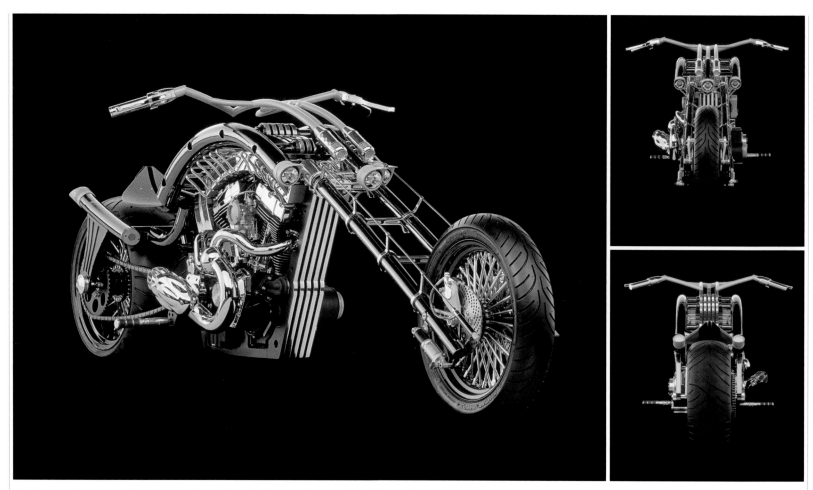

the future of custom choppers—a shape inspired by the aggressive stance of an angry praying mantis."

The $250,000 Rapture has a frame machined from a solid block of aircraft-grade T6 aluminium that weighed 900 lb (198 kg) before being whittled down to just 100 lb (45 kg) by engineering wizard Nagel. The fantastical creation scooped the $10,000 Best of Show prize on its first public appearance at the Los Angeles Calendar Motorcycle Show in the summer of 2005.

"Like all our bikes, the Rapture was constructed from both existing components and entirely created designs that sprang from a clean sheet of paper," says Nagel. "This latter part of the design process is sanctified by extensive research in both forms and materials to express beauty as well as strength. Thus, the creative process expressed in existing components—such as the powertrain—versus new creation, is expressed in the pricing of each individual machine."

Along with their concept motorcycle, Dreamcraft customers also receive all the artwork used to create it, from initial sketches to component drawings and computer files, as well as a video recording of the machine being built from the ground up.

Just as the Discovery Channel brought Orange County Choppers into the limelight, so Dreamcraft is heading that way through a broadcaster called Rolling Art Television, which aims to feature Nagel and Yang in a stand-alone series to be broadcast around the world.

And here's a prediction: before long we'll see a Dreamcraft production coming under the hammer in one of the high-rolling contemporary auctions staged by Christie's or Sotheby's. After all, Dreamcraft describes its products as "rolling works of art" and who could disagree that those words are entirely fair and accurate?

Above and opposite
The Dreamcraft DCS–001 Saga: the machine that brought Nagel and Yang international recognition.

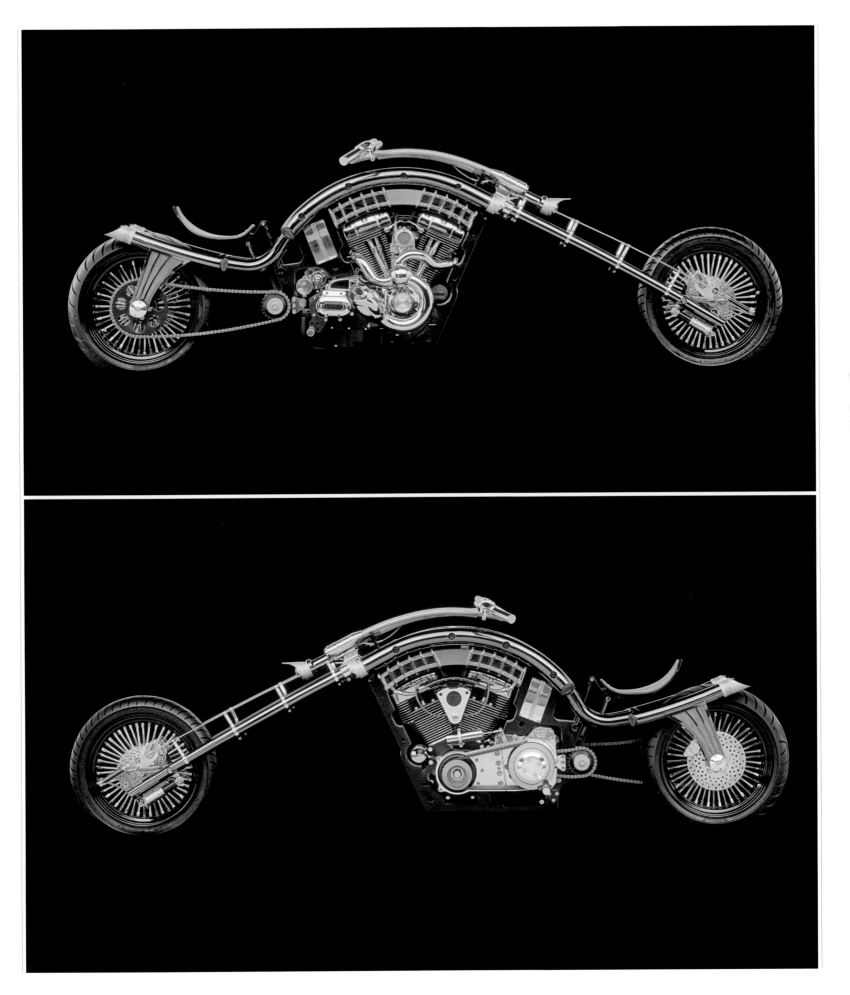

ERIK BUELL
Buell

By rights there shouldn't be a Buell in *The New Motorcycle Yearbook*. Not because Buell machines don't cut the mustard—far from it—but because the firm's founder, Erik Buell, was chasing a dream when he single-handedly built his first machine and, as a rule, dreams don't come true.

In Buell's case, however, his vision of creating powerful, fine-handling motorcycles based on a passion for form and function rather than the sound commerce of a bean counter's calculations turned to reality in a remarkably successful way.

Bikes have been in Buell's blood since he was twelve, when he first rode a friend's Honda Super Cub around the country lanes of Gibsonia, Pennsylvania, where he was born into a family of farmers. The young Buell learned to mend agricultural machinery and grew up fascinated by mechanical things, so motorcycles were an obvious draw. His first was an Italian Perilla moped, but he soon graduated to a Harley-Davidson chopper (which he bought as a basket case and rebuilt), then a racing Velocette and various Japanese road bikes.

By his late teens Buell was working as a part-time mechanic for an amateur road racer. Before long he took to the track himself and immediately became hooked. However, his unstoppable urge to race required considerable funds, so when he graduated from night school with a degree in mechanical engineering in 1979, he immediately flew to Milwaukee and, in his words, "talked his way into a job" as a junior test engineer at the then far from healthy Harley-Davidson company.

In his free time Buell raced Yamaha and Ducati bikes but, naturally enough, he felt somewhat guilty about not being on a homegrown Harley, particularly since the great American firm was going through troubled times. The problem was, of course, that Harley-Davidson didn't make a race bike.

Before long Buell had built his own racer, using an engine and chassis from the tiny Wales-based manufacturer Barton. The engine, which was extremely powerful, blew up while it was being warmed through in the pits, but once that was fixed the chassis quickly proved itself to be entirely inadequate.

At that stage most people would have given up trying to compete with the expertise and resources of the top Japanese and Italian manufacturers, but not Buell. He believed in the basic design of the Barton and believed, too, that it only needed to be tweaked and refined to become a good-quality competitive machine. So when the company went bust, he was first in the line to buy its inventory and set up his own, eponymous firm making motorcycles.

"The first official Buell was called the RW750, a two-stroke, square-four, rotary valve monster," recalls Buell. "It had power to spare and wildly different-looking aerodynamic bodywork. The RW stood for "Road Warrior," reflecting my sense of being a lone foot soldier waging war against the motorcycle giants of the world."

Against all the odds, the RW750, which produced a remarkable 123 kW (165 bhp) at the crankshaft, showed it had the potential to outperform the opposition and

> **"The first official Buell was called the RW750 .... The RW stood for 'Road Warrior', reflecting my sense of being a lone foot soldier waging war against the motorcycle giants of the world."**
> Erik Buell

Above
Buell's latest creation—the XB12 Lightning
Long—offers greater long-distance comfort
and stability than the standard, short-
wheelbase machine but still handles sharply.

Buell rode it to several wins at club level before a rule change by the American Motorcycle Association rendered the bike "illegal" and therefore unsaleable.

Next came the RR1000 Battletwin, which was, perhaps, the first Buell based on the philosophy around which all the firm's machines are now designed: the so-called "trilogy of technology," which combines mass centralization with chassis rigidity and low unsprung weight to enhance handling and response.

Buell sold fifty examples of the RR racer before the AMA changed the rules once again, at which stage he "decided it was time to concentrate on the street." Using the RR frame fitted with Harley-Davidson's then new 1203-cc Evolution engine, the bikes began to trickle out to buyers: sixty-five of the first model were sold during 1989, while the later Westwind, available fully faired or as a single-seater, sold 325 in three years. By 1993 the Buell name was starting to be recognized.

"Sales were beyond my wildest dreams. Halfway through the production of the RR we moved out of my garage, where all the work was being done, to a small facility in Mukwonago, Wisconsin. By 1991 we were able not only to design bodywork but to produce it, too, which gave us greater quality control and flexibility.

"The distinctive styling of the bikes and the clean lines gained the attention of the motorcycle press but, equally importantly, my former employer and long-time engine supplier Harley-Davidson also began to show an interest in the fledgling company."

As a result, a 49% stake in the Buell Motorcycle Company was sold to Harley-Davidson in 1993, enabling Buell to reinvest in a business that now had the backing of one of the best-known names in the world.

The Thunderbolt S2 appeared the following year, wowing the world with its distinctive looks and innovative design—not to mention the roar of the stubby muffler mounted centrally beneath the engine that has since become a Buell calling card. But the real draw of the Thunderbolt was that it was the first widely available sports bike America had ever produced. Around 1700 were sold, together with more than 400 sports-touring versions, at which stage Buell found its true niche, with the introduction of the radical Lightning in 1995–96.

This was Buell's first "streetfighter" motorcycle, which boasted an exposed frame and short tail section that gave it the aggressive stance that custom-bike builders the world over had been striving for when they performed backyard conversions on such machines as the Suzuki GSX-R750 and the Yamaha Diversion.

The difference with the Lightning, however, was that it was an integrated design concept with an engine suspended from the frame to reduce vibration, unsprung weight kept to a minimum, and as much sprung weight as possible kept low and central—among its many awards was one for Best Hooligan Motorcycle. The torquey Harley-Davidson v-twin engine combined with the short, quick-handling chassis made for off-the-throttle wheelies and enormous back-road fun, while the slim lines and small dimensions of the bike made it practical in town.

The slightly more relaxed Cyclone followed, then the White Lightning S1W of 1998, which was powered by the Thunderstorm, a special Harley-Davidson engine tuned to produce more than 75 kW (100 bhp).

Yet it was the comparatively tame, entry-level Blast—a 492-cc, single-cylinder machine—that, in 2000, pushed Buell's annual sales beyond the 9000 mark for the first time, despite few of its machines having been sold outside America.

The bike was instigated by Harley-Davidson bigwigs, who, in 1998, had bought a further 49% stake in Buell, to become the majority stockholder, leaving Erik Buell with a 2% share in the company, as chairman and chief technical officer. "That freed me up to concentrate on my personal vision for the motorcycles and less on day-to-day business matters," he says. "The company was growing like never before but our design philosophy was still there and we continued to look for ways to break new ground and expand the market. While so many manufacturers seemed fixated on speed and raw power, my ideal was a bike that would become one with the rider and make the riding experience an intuitive fusion of body, bike, and road—and that was the Firebolt XB9R."

Buell admits that some of the ideas that made it into production on the XB9R at first seemed "crazy," such as the lightweight frame that doubles as a fuel tank, the swing arm, which is also an engine oil reservoir, and the ultrashort wheelbase and steep steering angle that give the bike the dimensions of a Grand Prix racer, rather than a road-going superbike.

Other radical touches included Buell's use of what he calls a "Zero Torsion Load" front brake, in which the rotor, or disc, is mounted on the outside of the wheel rim so that the wheel spokes no longer have to carry torsional braking loads. This means they can be made lighter to greatly reduce unsprung weight.

The Lightning XB9S and XB12S (the second with the larger-capacity 1200-cc engine) joined the range in 2003 and, as readers of The New Motorcycle Yearbook 1 will know, 2005 saw the introduction of the Lightning City XB9SX, a machine very much designed to take on all that the urban jungle has to throw at it.

Now Buell has surprised us all again with the rugged-looking Ulysses, which can be found in the Adventure Sports section of this book.

But has the seemingly unstoppable growth of a firm that started out with one man in his garage with a pile of unwanted Welsh motorcycle parts altered Buell's original vision? The answer, it seems, is no, for he says: "Seeing Buell grow from a one-man band to a large, successful motorcycle manufacturer has not, I'm pleased to say, diminished my ability to create—that was something I worried about, but we've proved that the more people we have, the more creativity we have to work with. I'm having a ton of fun."

Above left
Erik Buell astride a Firebolt XB9R.
Above and opposite
The Buell Ulysses is intended to be swift on the highway and capable on the dirt.

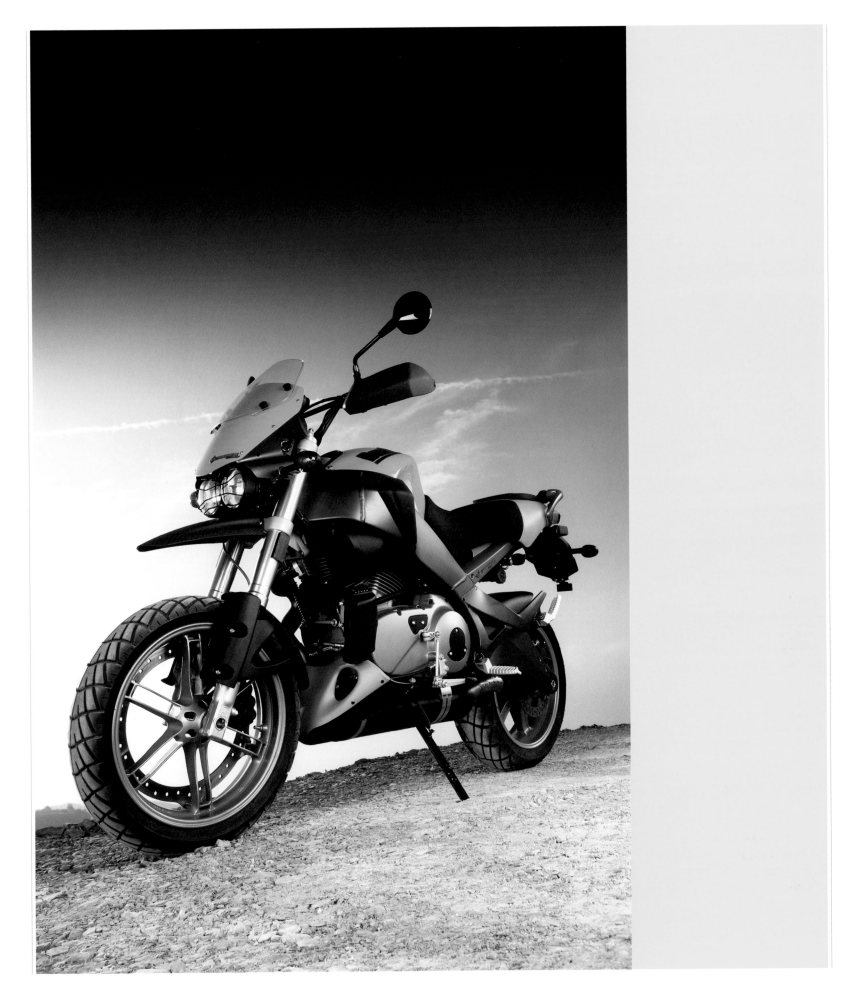

CCM

If ever you get to visit the CCM factory, don't bother looking for a door marked "design department" because there isn't one. Yet it was a brand-new CCM design that provoked more attention than any other make at the 2005 International Motorcycle Show in Birmingham, UK.

The CCM FT35 is a niche bike, a "flat-tracker" produced by a small factory in correspondingly small numbers but, in the world of motorcycle design, great oaks from little acorns grow. And it won't be the first time that this firm has set the ball rolling, with not just a new style of bike but a whole new genre of motorcycling.

Toward the end of the 1990s, CCM was instrumental in establishing the craze for road-legal supermoto machines when it launched a motorcycle equipped with top-quality motocross components and fitted with a 598-cc, four-stroke Rotax engine, lights, and turn signals.

No manufacturer had produced such a machine, although the fact that plenty of owners had attempted to execute the concept in their own garages demonstrated that a market for one clearly existed. Naturally, CCM's lead was quickly followed and now there are numerous supermoto models available, ranging from the hard-core products of such firms as KTM, to the more diluted, street-oriented bikes made by Honda, Yamaha, and the like.

The fact is, it is often the small manufacturers close to the grass roots of motorcycling that produce radical designs that then go on to inspire much larger companies to interpret them in their own way and to market them to the world as the latest "must-have" motorcycles. For this reason we can expect to see street-legal flat-track-style machines from the major manufacturers in the near future.

What is perhaps most extraordinary in CCM's case, however, is that it was just six months before the FT35 and its supermoto cousin the R35 were unveiled that the previously dormant company announced its return to motorcycle production—remember, the major manufacturers are already working on their models for 2010 and beyond.

CCM is an entirely British make that has experienced various ups and downs since it was established in 1971, including several changes of ownership. Its previous owners put the company into liquidation in July 2004, an event that its many fans expected would be the final chapter in its history.

However, in May 2005 the firm's founder, Alan Clews, bought back all of CCM's assets at the age of sixty-eight and, together with his son Austin and son-in-law Gary Harthern, announced that CCM would bounce back with a new and exciting range of single-cylinder, four-stroke motorcycles.

The team's first task was to get together and start designing, using the frame and suspension components that they had acquired with the buyback of the CCM name. "There are only seven of us in the entire company, so designing a new bike literally involves sitting around a table with some pieces of paper and putting together a few ideas," said Austin. "As a very small company we

"There are only seven of us in the company, so designing a new bike literally involves sitting around a table with some pieces of paper and putting together a few ideas."
Austin Clews

Opposite
CCM founder Alan Clews on a 1980s Scrambler.
Above
The Royal Signals motorcycle display team —aka The White Helmets—used CCM machines for its more radical stunts.

have to try to think at least one step ahead of the big manufacturers the whole time in order to be able to offer something different. That is what we did in the late 1990s when we found our trail bikes were facing huge competition from everyone else. To counter that, we developed the first street-legal supermoto bikes and, before too long, many other firms followed suit.

"That meant we had to think of something else again, and so we came up with the Flat Tracker. There is a new flat-track-racing series taking off in the UK and we believe that, as it gains momentum, the popularity of this style of bike will increase among road riders. For us, designing a bike such as that simply means getting on with the job after our normal day's work has been done—so we meet up in the evenings and at weekends and, when we think we have a concept, employ an artist to produce a cohesive image and bring it all to life."

Flat-track racing is most common in America, where the sport has been thrilling crowds since the 1920s. Until the arrival of the FT35, the nearest machine to a flat-track racer that you could buy off the shelf was a special version of Harley-Davidson's Sportster, which, in reality, is simply a cosmetic makeover and a far cry from the legendary XR racers, which are said to be the most successful competition motorcycles of all time.

Honda, too, collaborated with motorcycle-mad clothes designer Nick Ashley (son of the late Laura Ashley) to come up with a flat-track-style machine that was produced in very limited numbers, mainly for sale in Japan.

The FT35, however, is both a genuine race bike (it is available as the FT35R for track use) and a practical road bike that also has the mean, pared-down looks that are essential flat-tracker features. Powered by a 400-cc, liquid-cooled Suzuki engine, it combines reliability in daily use with the exclusivity of custom components, including its beautiful, hand-beaten aluminum fuel tank and barking, upswept exhaust system.

Despite its small size, CCM has long been regarded as Britain's "second" motorcycle manufacturer after Triumph, which is now in a totally different league, after posting a 45% rise in sales during the first six months of 2005 and profits of £10.7 million, an increase of more than £9 million in a year. Yet to a whole generation of motorcyclists—me included—CCM is just as important a name as Triumph.

Alan Clews started out in 1971, making his first BSA-engined motorcycles in his home garage before moving the business the following year to production premises at Jubilee Works in Bolton, Lancashire— coincidentally the site of the reborn CCM factory today—where he first registered the CCM name. It was not long before the thunderous sound of CCM scramblers was being heard on Britain's national television network, thanks to the regular weekend broadcasts by ITN Sport of the country's motocross events.

Such star riders as John Banks, Vic Eastwood and Bob Wright successfully raced CCMs as far afield as Finland and Canada, and in 1977 Eddie Kidd used a

CCM motocross bike to perform the first-ever leap over thirteen double-decker buses.

By the early 1980s, when the Armstrong Group acquired part-ownership, CCM was proving a competitive force in road racing, with bikes taking first, third and fourth places in the 1981 Isle of Man Junior TT, ridden by Steve Tonkin, and first, fourth, and fifth places in the 1985 British Road Race Championship, ridden by Niall Mackenzie. Trials success followed, too, with Steve Saunders riding a CCM to victory in the 1985 British Trials Championship.

That same year, the firm was awarded the Queen's Award for Export after signing a contract to produce 4000 motorcycles with the Can Am emblem for sale in North America. And in 1987 (at which stage CCM was again wholly owned by the Clews family) it produced more than 3000 military machines for supply to the British, Canadian, and Jordanian armies, prompting Harley-Davidson to buy the manufacturing design and rights to build the MT500 in the USA.

Now well and truly back in the driver's seat, Alan Clews is once more looking to the future of the firm he founded all those years ago and too often became disconnected from. "Building bikes is not just a business, it's a way of life, something that is with you twenty-four hours a day, seven days a week," he says. "If you are only focused on profit then this is not the business to be in. When I sold CCM I believed it was the right thing to do, as the new owners had access to the investment that I felt would help take it forward.

"While the company did benefit in some ways it also, unfortunately, had its heart ripped out as the new management had no passion for what CCM stood for. Now it is back in our control we want to bring back the values that worked so well for us previously.

"We will concentrate on quality rather than quantity, and we will, once again, use our racing heritage to design some new, niche models that will bring back some great nostalgia—but, all-importantly, with a modern twist."

Above
An original design for the CCM FT35.

Left, top to bottom, and above
All flat-track and supermoto machines in the CCM range are hand built.
Below
Former World Superbike Champion Carl Fogarty puts a CCM through its paces on the track.

MOTORCYCLE TYPES

TOURERS

Thirty years ago the hardened long-distance rider had little choice of motorcycle. BMW's shaft-drive, flat-twins had carved out a niche as definitive touring machines and Honda was starting to offer competition, with its luxurious, water-cooled Gold Wing. These apart, it was a matter of throwing a set of panniers over your faithful all-round vehicle and heading for the hills.

Today it is a very different story, with every serious manufacturer offering superbly equipped, large-engined, purpose-built touring bikes that are as well appointed as some family cars.

Aerodynamically efficient fairings protect rider and passenger from the elements at three-figure cruising speeds, ergonomically designed seats ensure daylong comfort and intercom-linked sound systems relieve highway monotony. Handlebar grips (and seats) are invariably heated, fuel tanks can offer a range of more than 250 miles (402 km) and modular luggage systems that lock on to purpose-built carrying racks provide capacious, stylish, secure storage.

SPORTS BIKES

The ability of motorcycle manufacturers to transfer one year's racetrack experience to the next year's model range is extraordinary. Two-wheeled race technology reaches the road far more quickly than comparable advances in the car world, so much so that most road-going machines have the brakes, power, and handling to make them competitive racers straight from the crate.

Huge leaps in engineering mean that 600-cc engines are now producing more power than the one-liter units of the 1980s, and extensive use of aluminum, magnesium, titanium and carbon fiber results in chassis that are light and rigid.

Combined with twenty-first-century suspension and tire and braking technology, this makes for superb-handling machines that are blindingly fast. At the same time, clever electronic mapping of fuel and ignition systems ensures that a motorcycle capable of 180 mph (290 km/h) can still be relied upon to behave itself in city traffic.

As for comfort, you can forget it. Sports bikes are uncompromising racetrack refugees that demand a jockey crouch from the rider and come into their own on a ribbon of twisting blacktop where pillion passengers just don't belong.

SUPERMOTOS

Whoever thought of combining a motocross track with short stretches of metaled race circuit created an entirely new category of motorcycle that has taken the two-wheeled world by storm.

Supermotos are what you get when you put a set of wide wheels with sticky road tires on to an off-road motorcycle. The latest models shamelessly bring out the hooligan in every rider. Firm, long-travel suspension, wasp-slim dimensions, monster disc brakes and, most importantly, a big-bore, four-stroke, single-cylinder engine put the fun back into motorcycling.

Many buyers are converted former sports-bike riders who find a supermoto can fulfil their need for thrills with its lightning handling, punchy, wheelie-prone engine, and the type of stopping power that will easily stand the machine on its nose. Most of these bikes have a top speed of around 80 mph (129 km/h), which makes it harder for overeager riders to lose their licenses, and, as well as making great commuter machines, they offer an inexpensive way into competition, for supermoto racing provides thrill-a-minute fun on tight, twisty kart tracks.

TRAIL BIKES

A trail (not trails, trial or trials) bike is a road-going motorcycle with off-road capability. It has a softly tuned engine, compliant, long-travel suspension, decent ground clearance and, usually, room for a passenger. A trail bike, therefore, is not an all-out off-road racing machine, but a machine that is just as at home on a tree-lined lane in the country as it is when used for commuting in the city.

The most popular trail bikes used to have an engine capacity of 250 cc or less. Usually two-strokes, they were light, nimble and easy to drag out of a muddy ditch. Now, stricter emission rules and the mass use of lightweight materials have led to the quieter, cleaner four-stroke engine being more favored. A 250-cc, four-stroke trail bike is now lighter, niftier and more forgiving than the two-strokes of old, and most are equipped with suspension systems that, not so long ago, would have been found only on state-of-the-art motocross racers.

ENDURO BIKES

Enduro motorcycles are similar to trail bikes, only more competition-oriented and sometimes nothing more than road-legal motocrossers. An enduro is a type of off-road trial in which competitors are required to cover large distances over difficult terrain against the clock.

CRUISERS

Harley-Davidson started it all with its large-capacity, laid-back, v-twin groundshakers that remain the stuff of dreams and legend. The company is the world's most successful producer of cruiser bikes, but competition continues to hot up in a category of machine that many riders believe epitomizes the freedom of motorcycling.

A cruiser doesn't need to be fast; it just needs to have presence. The v-twin engine has emerged as the classic powerplant, and the larger the capacity the better. Make the frame long and low, make the handlebars wide and high, and put the footrests well forward. Pad the saddle and add plenty of chrome, a fat back tire and exhausts as mean-sounding as the law will allow. Then you've got a cruiser.

Buyers are often "born-again" bikers with cash to spend, who like the low seat height and loping gait that cruisers offer. The latest bikes handle surprisingly well, too, and with a range of models from every maker, it no longer has to be a Harley—although for cruiser purists, it does really.

ADVENTURE SPORTS

When manufacturers such as BMW, Yamaha and Honda introduced their first big four-stroke trail machines in the early 1980s, riders discovered a whole new world of motorcycling. They found that these large, comfortable machines were ideal for exploring difficult-to-reach parts of the world. Their off-road credentials meant they could ford rivers and cross deserts, their lazy engines provided an adequate cruising speed, and their imposing size gave them the luggage-carrying ability of a small camel.

Spring-loaded gear and brake levers, flexible indicator stems and lightweight, plastic mudguards protected them from the knocks and bumps of unpaved roads, and large-capacity fuel tanks lessened the problem of the lack of filling stations in remote areas.

These motorcycles heralded today's adventure sports machines, more of which are now sold than any other category of motorcycle. The latest have powerful, twin-cylinder engines, bikini fairings blended into their fuel tanks and unfeasibly sharp handling. With numerous aftermarket accessories available to enhance their considerable capability for adventure, they have truly made the world a smaller place.

SPORTS TOURERS

What we call a "sports tourer" nowadays would, not so long ago, have been regarded as a hypersports race replica. The power and handling of these machines leaves old-school sports bikes for dead, yet they also manage to be surprisingly practical.

With less radical riding positions than their more uncompromising pure sports cousins, sports tourers accommodate rider and passenger in reasonable comfort over long distances. A wealth of luggage has been designed to fit around their curvaceous flanks and tanks, yet the sleek appearance of the average sports bike won't leave would-be racers feeling embarrassed that they are not riding the real thing.

In fact, for those willing to admit that all-out sports bikes are too uncomfortable and needlessly fast for daily use, sports tourers such as Honda's VFR 800 and Triumph's Sprint ST have come to be regarded as true all-round vehicles.

STREET BIKES

Street bikes are best described as "traditional" motorcycles: not glamorous, not especially sporty, not madly fast, and not always state-of-the-art. These are machines based on tried-and-tested engineering, sometimes slightly old-fashioned looks and the simple principle of motorcycle as workhorse. Engines range in size from 250 cc to 750 cc and the bikes sell to commuter riders who appreciate their reliability and lack of pretension.

NAKED BIKES

No sooner had the first sports bikes emerged during the early 1980s than riders were ripping off the fairings, junking the dropped handlebars in favor of upright ones, and creating mean-looking "streetfighter"-style custom bikes that exposed once more the artwork of engineering.

Twenty years later and the major manufacturers are making streetfighters, now commonly called "naked" bikes, the likes of which the DIY customizers of the 1980s could only have dreamed of.

Usually derived from pure sports models, they offer an upright riding position that makes them more practical for everyday riding, yet their engines are only mildly detuned and, with their state-of-the-art sports suspension, they handle equally well. Aggressive twin exhausts tucked beneath seats, fat tires and unconventionally shaped headlamps are currently *de rigueur* on nakeds.

It is hard to believe that the mean looks of the latest nakeds could ever be improved upon, but in reality, of course, they surely will be.

MUSCLE BIKES

Muscle bikes follow the same basic principles as street bikes but derive their description from the large-capacity, multi-cylinder engines that power them. Consequently, they are big machines with significant presence and they require a fair amount of muscle to handle.

Models such as Suzuki's Bandit 1200, Yamaha's XJR1300, and Kawasaki's ZRX1200 have been around for years now, but they continue to have a strong following among riders who like a motorcycle to look like a motorcycle and who appreciate the bulletproof engines and comfortable, upright riding positions that muscle bikes offer.

RETROS

There are plenty of older motorcyclists who regard some of the British and Italian machines of the 1970s through rose-tinted goggles; but the fact is, although they looked like rolling works of art, many of these bikes were less than reliable.

Motorcycle technology has progressed by leaps and bounds since then. The electrics are better, engines are more powerful, more efficient and more reliable, and the materials and methods used in frame building make modern chassis that are lighter, stronger, and more rigid.

Imagine if those great-looking old bikes had been this good. Well, it seems, they can be now. Firms such as Triumph and Ducati have produced modern-day versions of the 1970s classics and managed to bring the style we love right up to date in a modern package. Royal Enfield is back, too, with a modernized version of the Bullet equipped with electric start and five gears.

SCOOTERS

The word "scooter" used to refer only to the instantly recognizable Vespas, Lambrettas and the like, which have become as much a part of Italian culture as pizza and ice cream, but modern scooters come in all shapes and sizes and from manufacturers all over the world. An unwritten rule seems to dictate that once a scooter's engine exceeds 250 cc it becomes a "maxi" or "super" scooter, but otherwise anything goes.

The main features of a scooter are that it has a platform and leg shields rather than exposed footrests, its engine is enclosed, and invariably it has "twist and go" transmission, which makes it easy and convenient to ride. Underseat storage space is also desirable and, whereas small wheels were once universal, many scooter riders prefer the added stability provided by the larger rims often found on the latest models.

MAXI SCOOTERS

Three-figure maximum speeds, single-figure 0–60-mph (0–97 km/h) times and relaxed long-distance cruising ability were at one time never associated with scooters, because they had small engines and tiny wheels and worked best in strictly urban environments, but the emergence of the first maxi scooters in the late 1990s changed attitudes toward their predecessors. They took the automatic, twist-and-go ease of scooter riding to a new level, with their half-litre engines, aerodynamic fairings and bigger wheels. Maxi scooters can carry two in comfort and mix it in the highway fast lane with confidence; they're even good for touring.

Practicality, however, is the crux of the maxi scooter. These machines offer a useful amount of storage space, their protective bodywork means you need not turn up at the office looking disheveled, and the most sophisticated models boast features such as heated handlebars, stereo systems, electrically adjustable screens and mobile-telephone chargers.

ODDBALLS

As components become cheaper and easier to produce, consumers demand new forms of entertainment, and as conventions become ever more irrelevant, motorcycle designers become all the more imaginative.

So it's no surprise that a new, unclassifiable form of powered two-wheeler is emerging that has been strongly influenced by skateboard and BMX culture. These bikes take knocks and bumps in their stride, ooze street cred and, in some cases, can be used to perform far-out stunts.

Included in the Oddballs section of this book you will find everything from a high-performance electric scooter to a stunt bike that is so pared down it is almost more bicycle than motorbike. There is even one machine powered by a helicopter engine and a Harley-Davidson dragster that can be bought off the shelf and ready to race.

GLOSSARY

Italics indicate a cross-reference.

AIRBOX
A chamber attached to a *carburetor* or fuel-injection system through which air is supplied to enable vaporization of fuel to take place. Also acts as a housing for the *air filter*.

AIR COOLING
Air-cooled engines rely on the passage of air to dissipate heat from around the engine and, usually, are heavily finned for this purpose.

AIR FILTER
A foam or corrugated-card device that prevents airborne foreign matter, such as dust and water, from entering the fuel-delivery system.

ANTILOCK BRAKING SYSTEM (ABS)
A system to prevent loss of control caused by a wheel locking on slippery surfaces or under extreme braking. ABS electronically releases and restores braking pressure at intervals of fractions of a second to prevent wheel locking.

BASH PLATE
Protective metal guard often used on off-road or dual-purpose machines to prevent damage to the underside of the motorcycle engine by stones and other debris.

BELT DRIVE
A clean and quiet method of transferring power from the gearbox to the driven wheel via a flexible toothed belt, as opposed to a chain or driveshaft. Particularly favored by Harley-Davidson.

BHP (BRAKE HORSEPOWER)
The imperial unit of measurement of the power developed by an engine. The corresponding metric unit is the kilowatt (kW) (1 bhp = 0.7457 kW).

BORE
The diameter of an individual *cylinder* in an engine, inside which the piston travels.

CALIPER
The part of a *disc brake* that presses brake pads on to the brake disc to slow the wheel.

CAMSHAFT
The part of an engine that controls the opening and closing of the inlet and exhaust valves that draw in vaporized fuel and expel spent gases. Many motorcycles have *double overhead camshafts*.

CAPACITY
A measure of engine size, referred to as "cc" (cubic centimetres). A 1-litre engine is described as "1000 cc." This is also measured in cubic inches (1 cubic in. = 16.4 cc).

CARBON FIBER
A very light and strong material made of woven and bonded carbon that is often used to produce ancillary parts for high-performance motorcycles.

CARBURETOR
A device that mixes fuel and air in the correct quantities and feeds it into an engine to enable internal combustion.

CASSETTE GEARBOX
A modular gear cluster that can quickly be removed from a motorcycle engine and replaced with an alternative set of gears to give different ratios. Most useful on race machines.

CAST-ALLOY WHEEL
A popular type of motorcycle wheel that is light, strong and easy to clean, and can be produced in many styles.

CLUTCH
A component that converts the power of an engine into drive to the *transmission*. The "slipper" clutch, currently popular on sports bikes, eliminates the danger of the rear wheel locking during downward gear changes at high engine revs.

COMPRESSION RATIO
The ratio of maximum *cylinder* to combustion chamber volume, when the piston is at the top of its stroke, compared with when it is at the bottom of its stroke.

CON(NECTING) ROD
A part of an engine connecting the rotating *crankshaft* to the piston in order to convert rotation into vertical or horizontal movement.

CRANKCASE
A casing containing the *crankshaft* and gearbox.

CRANKSHAFT
A rotating shaft to which the *connecting rod(s)* is attached.

CYLINDER
A cylindrical chamber in which a piston travels.

CYLINDER HEAD
The "head" of an engine, containing inlet and exhaust valves and, in an overhead-camshaft engine, the *camshaft*.

DESMODROMIC
A system of valve control used by Ducati, in which a cam, not a spring, opens and closes the engine's valves.

DISC BRAKE
A brake that operates by pressing pads of friction material on to a disc attached to the wheel.

DOUBLE OVERHEAD CAMSHAFT
Usually found in high-performance engines. Two *camshafts* enable the inlet and exhaust valves to be closed and opened more efficiently.

DRUM BRAKE
A brake that operates pressing "shoes" of friction material on to a cylindrical wall inside a wheel hub.

DRY SUMP
A lubrication system that stores oil in a separate tank, rather than in a sump at the bottom of the engine. Common in racing motorcycles, it prevents a surge of oil during hard braking, accelerating and cornering.

DRY WEIGHT
The weight of a motorcycle without fuel, oil or coolant.

DYNAMOMETER
A machine used to measure engine *torque*, enabling brake horsepower to be calculated.

ELECTRONIC FUEL INJECTION (EFI)
A more efficient but more complicated method of supplying vaporized fuel to the combustion chamber than a *carburetor*.

ENDURO
A type of off-road competition in which riders follow an unseen course in a specified time.

ENGINE BRAKING
The braking effect of an engine when the *throttle* is closed; this is particularly strong on large-capacity, *v-twin* engines.

FLAT-TWIN
An engine configuration in which the two *cylinders* are horizontally opposed to each other. Also known as "boxer" configuration.

FLICKABILITY
A colloquial term used to describe the ease with which a motorcycle can be made to change direction at speed; best assessed by riding through a series of sweeping bends.

FOUR-STROKE
An engine that requires four piston strokes per power stroke.

GAS FLOWING
The act of modifying the inlet and exhaust ports of a *cylinder head* in order to improve the flow of fuel vapour into the engine and the exit of exhaust gasses.

GEARTRAIN
The system of gears, chains and/or shafts that transmit power from the engine's *crankshaft* to the driven wheel.

GP
Acronym for Grand Prix.

HORIZONTALLY OPPOSED
An engine configuration in which the *cylinders* are opposed at 180 degrees to one another.

HUB
The central part of a wheel.

HUGGER
A type of close-fitting rear-wheel mudguard.

INJECTOR
A pressurized nozzle through which a fuel-injection system feeds vaporized fuel into the combustion chamber.

INVERTED FORKS
Front suspension system in which the sliders (the thick sections of the forks) are at the top rather than at the bottom. Inverted forks are currently considered state-of-the-art and are found mainly on high-performance motorcycles, although Suzuki has recently used them on one of its cruiser bikes.

KICK-STARTER
An integral, foot-operated crank used to start a motorcycle's engine.

LEADING LINK
A type of front suspension in which the wheel spindle is mounted ahead of a pivoted link.

LIQUID COOLING
A method of maintaining an even engine temperature by passing water around the engine through a water jacket linked to a radiator cooled by the flow of air. Also known as *water cooling*.

LONG-STROKE
A term used to describe an engine in which the stroke, or the vertical travel of the piston, exceeds the *bore* of the *cylinder*.

L-TWIN
An engine configuration in which the *cylinders* are arranged in an "L" shape, i.e., at, or almost at, a right angle to each other. A typical example is the Ducati twin-cylinder engine, in which the angle between the *cylinders* is too great for the configuration to be described as "V."

MARQUE
An alternative word for make, e.g. BMW, Ducati, and Triumph.

OIL COOLING
A method of cooling an engine whereby lubricating oil passes through a radiator. It is used as an additional means of cooling both *air-* and *liquid-cooled* engines.

OVERBORED
A term used to describe an engine of which the *capacity* has been increased beyond its original size.

OVER-SQUARE
A term used to describe an engine in which the *bore* is greater than the stroke, a feature of most modern, high-revving, multicylinder motorcycle engines.

PANNIER
Rear-mounted luggage item that is made either of a hard material, such as glass fiber, or of a soft, water-resistant material.

PEAKY
A term used to describe an engine that has a narrow *power band* at high revs and makes little power at lower revs.

POWER BAND
The point in the rev range at which an engine makes its maximum potential power. This is usually somewhat lower than the maximum safe rev limit.

POWERTRAIN
A term that encompasses the engine, gearbox and final-drive units of a motorcycle.

RADIAL BRAKE CALIPER
A brake *caliper* that is fitted by means of bolts running from back to front, rather than from one side to the other, to produce a more equal spread of pressure on the brake pads.

RAM AIR INTAKE
A scoop built into the fairing that is designed to force air into the machine's fuel system at speed, to improve combustion.

REGENERATIVE BRAKING
A system for transferring the kinetic energy produced under braking to electricity used to recharge the machine's batteries.

REV COUNTER
An instrument that measures the revolutions of an engine, usually in thousands per minute. Also known as a tachometer.

ROADABLE
A word used to describe the abilities of a dual-purpose machine on tarmac. A well-designed adventure sports bike, for example, will be capable of crossing a mountain pass but will also perform well on a highway, meaning it is still "roadable."

ROLL ON
The *capacity* of a motorcycle travelling at low engine revs in a high gear to accelerate rapidly and smoothly in the same gear using the engine's *torque*.

RPM
Revolutions per minute.

SHOCK ABSORBER
A term commonly used to describe a rear suspension unit or units.

SIAMESED
A term used to describe an exhaust system on a motorcycle with two or more *cylinders* in which individual exhaust pipes exiting from the engine merge together, usually ending in a single silencer.

SILENCER
A component of an exhaust system that muffles engine noise.

SLIDER
The moving part of a motorcycle fork.

SPARK PLUG
A component used to carry a spark across two electrodes inside an engine's combustion chamber to cause ignition. Twin-plug engines are currently popular for their greater efficiency and lower emissions.

SPEEDOMETER
An instrument used to measure speed of travel.

SPOKED WHEEL
The traditional type of motorcycle wheel, laced with a network of thin wire spokes. Particularly popular on off-road machines because individual spokes break on impact with hard objects and so provide a degree of shock absorption that protects the rim from deformation. A cast-alloy wheel may fracture in this situation.

STEERING DAMPER
A telescopic friction device used to counter steering shake at high speed.

SUBFRAME
A separate, detachable part of a chassis at the rear of the main frame.

SUMP
An oil reservoir sited underneath or inside a *crankcase*.

SWING ARM
A chassis component that holds the rear wheel and pivots vertically to enable the operation of the suspension system.

THROTTLE
Term used to describe the handlebar control that regulates fuel flow to the engine, although more accurately it refers to the variable restriction in a *carburetor* or fuel-injection system.

TORQUE
A measure of the force applied to produce rotational movement, measured in foot pounds (ft lb) or Newton meters (Nm). The majority of the torque figures cited in this book are given in Newton meters (1.356 Nm = 1 ft lb). Engines that produce high torque figures at low revs have the best pulling power for hill climbing and can accelerate more smoothly from lower revs in a high gear than less "torquey" engines. Single- and twin-cylinder engines tend to be "torquey," whereas multicylinder engines tend to be "revvy."

TRANSMISSION
A system of gears by which engine power is transformed into drive.

UNSPRUNG WEIGHT
The part of an engine that lies beneath—i.e., on the road side—of the suspension, such as parts of the wheels, the brakes, and a portion of the suspension itself.

VALVE
A part of an engine that allows fuel to enter the combustion chamber and waste gases to exit it. Sophisticated, higher-revving engines have several valves in each *cylinder* (five in some Yamaha engines). A four-cylinder engine with four valves per *cylinder* is referred to as a sixteen-valve engine.

V-FOUR
V-four engines are usually arranged as two banks of *cylinders*, in "V" formation, placed side by side across the motorcycle frame.

V-TWIN
An engine configuration in which twin cylinders form a "V" shape. A typical example is a Harley-Davidson engine.

WATER COOLING
A method of maintaining an even engine temperature, by passing water around the engine through a water jacket linked to a radiator that is cooled by the flow of air. Also known as *liquid cooling*.

MOTORCYCLE SHOWS

SEPTEMBER 8–11, 2006
Eurobike, Friedrichshafen,
Germany

SEPTEMBER 14–17, 2006
IFMA, Cologne, Germany

SEPTEMBER 22–29, 2006
Mondial du deux-roues, Paris

OCTOBER 11–15, 2006
Intermot, Cologne, Germany

OCTOBER 27 – NOVEMBER 5, 2006
International Motorcycle and
Scooter Show, National Exhibition
Centre (NEC), Birmingham, UK

NOVEMBER 14–19, 2006
EICMA Moto, New Milan
Fairgrounds, Milan, Italy

NOVEMBER 17–19, 2006
Sydney Motorcycle Show, Sydney
Showgrounds, Sydney, Australia

DECEMBER 7–17, 2006
Bologna Motor Show, Bologna,
Italy

JANUARY 5–7, 2007
National Motorcycle Show,
G-Mex Centre, Manchester, UK

JANUARY 5–7, 2007
Calgary Motorcycle Show, Roundup
Centre, Stampede Park, Calgary,
Canada

JANUARY 12–14, 2007
Edmonton Motorcycle Show,
Northlands Park, Agricom,
Edmonton, Canada

JANUARY 12–22, 2007
European Motor Show, Brussels
Expo, Brussels, Belgium

JANUARY 19–21, 2007
Springfield Motorcycle Show, West
Springfield, Massachusetts, USA

JANUARY 25–28, 2007
Vancouver Motorcycle Show, Tradex
Exhibition Centre, Abbotsford BC,
Canada

JANUARY 28 – FEBRUARY 5, 2007
MCN London Motorcycle Show,
Alexandra Palace, London

FEBRUARY 2007
Moto Bike 2007, Expocentre of
Ukraine, Kiev

FEBRUARY 2–4, 2007
MP 07 Motorcycle Exhibition,
Helsinki Fair Centre, Finland

FEBRUARY 9–11, 2007
Quebec City Motorcycle Show,
Quebec, Canada

MARCH 2007
Scottish Motorcycle Show, Royal
Highland Centre, Midlothian, UK

MARCH 2–6, 2007
Salon de la Moto, Montreal, Canada

MARCH 30 – APRIL 1, 2007
International Cycle Show, Tianjin,
China

APRIL 28–29, 2007
International Classic Motorcycle
Show, Stafford, UK

JULY 15–16, 2007
LA Calendar Motorcycle Show, Los
Angeles, California, USA

OCTOBER 11–15, 2007
Intermot, Cologne, Germany

OCTOBER 27 – NOVEMBER 11, 2007
The 40th Tokyo Motor Show,
Makuhari Messe, Makuhari, Tokyo

NOVEMBER 1–11, 2007
International Motorcycle and
Scooter Show, National Exhibition
Centre (NEC), Birmingham, UK